1936-1986

'Our true intent is all for your delight'

— William Shakespeare
SKEGNESS HOLIDAY CAMP

Butlin's holiday savings stamps

Acknowledgements

With grateful thanks to the hundreds of Butlin's campers who contacted me, the Butlin's organisation and to the following for all their photographs, souvenirs and invaluable memories that made this book possible:
Barbara Levy, Shirley Lewis, Andy Ayliffe, Martin Pegg, Kath Greer, Don Scott-Reid, Butlins Ltd, Bobby Butlin, Colonel and Mrs Basil Brown, Kay Bury, Rene Bradford, Jack & Joyce Briggs, Harold Berens, Albert & Vi Brown, Roger Billington, The Beverly Sisters, Ron Blow, Titch Brey, Bob Chalk, E. Broom, Victor Bonatto, Jerry Cable, Bret Cresswell, Dorothy Coates, Stanley Carter, George Crane, Charlie Chester, Ian Carmichael, Peter Casson, Eddy Cunningham, Charlie Drake, John Cussons, Freddie Davis, Bet Dunstan, Dorothy Coates, Arthur English, Stan Edwards, Heather French, J. Fitzpatrick, Ken Farmer, Muriel Fairburn, Wally Goodman, Ronnie Goslin, Brian Grey, T Garner, Billy Hazard, Walter & Rose Hilton, Dolly & Peter Harmer, Stan Haines, Paddy Hope, Roy Hudd, Joan & Dean Hardy, Dr Geraint James, Irish & Paddy Jesson, Winston Kine, David Luvering, Dr Lockyer, Mr Leyton Lindsey, Olive Lynn, Charles Miller, Dizzie Mansell, Mary Merril, Rev Malkenson, Alice Mathews, Frances Maloney, Stan Morse, George Melly, Margaret Wilson, Wilfred Orange, Jimmy Perry, Dorothy Wilson, Tony Peers, Kathleen Parkinson, Terry Rainsford, Molly Rowntree, Ted Rogers, Mike Reid, Gladys Radcliffe, George Stone, Ron Stanway, Roy Scofield, Harry Simpson, Bob Stowe, Richard Stone, Helen Shapiro, Skegness Council, Skegness Standard, The Sun newspaper, Mike Smith, Don Trapnell, Frances Ullman, A. Webster, Trevor Watts, Winifred West, Allen Wildman, Jane Winston, Annie & Frank Watson, Ted Young.
And to these books: *The Billy Butlin Story, A Showman to the End*, by Sir Billy Butlin with Peter Dacre, published by Robson Books. ISBN 0-86051-168-5.
The Butlin Story, by Rex North, published by Jarrolds. *Big Charlie*, by J. H. Williams, published by Rupert Hart-Davis.
Rum Bum and Concertina, by George Melly, published by Weidenfeld & Nicolson. ISBN 297 77341 0.
Photographs taken and supplied by: James W. Goulding, The Sunday Times: Bognor Birdman and the Salvation Army, Popperfoto: VE day at Filey, Leslie Purvis. Butlins Ltd, Brian Garrick, BBC. *Hi De Hi* TV Series, Jill Drower; *Good Clean Fun, The story of Britain's first holiday camp* (ISBN 0 8508344) Arcadia Books and Butlin's campers.

Butlin time: Butlin's gave thousands of people a wonderful time. They remember the atmosphere and the events but not always the actual time and date that they took place. They have their own holiday 'Butlin Time' which may not always be correct. The date wasn't important to most Butlin's campers, just the fun and games.

TRANSWORLD PUBLISHERS LTD
61-63 Uxbridge Road,
London W5 5SA

TRANSWORLD PUBLISHERS (AUSTRALIA) PTY LTD
26 Harley Crescent, Condell Park,
NSW 2200

TRANSWORLD PUBLISHERS (NZ) LTD
Cnr. Moselle and Waipareira Aves,
Henderson, Auckland

Copyright © Sue Read 1986

Typeset by Type Generation

Production by Baker Mahaffy Ltd.

Published 1986 by Bantam Press,
a division of Transworld Publishers Ltd.

This edition specially produced for
The Leisure Circle Limited
by arrangement with
Bantam Press,
a division of Transworld Publishers Ltd

ISBN 0–593–01039–6

Printed in Great Britain by
R. J. Acford, Chichester

HELLO CAMPERS!

Sue Read

with Brian Haynes

With an introduction by Jimmy Perry,
Creator of *Hi-de-Hi*

THE
LEISURE
CIRCLE

'Get up Mr Brown, Get up Mrs Brown, enjoy yourselves, Maudy, Tom and Gerald, don't forget to read the *Daily Herald*. So get up Dad and Mum, the morning has come, Mr Butlin wishes you a happy day.'

Contents

INTRODUCTION

By Jimmy Perry creator and co-author with David Croft of the BBC-TV series *Hi-de-Hi*.

The Official Magazine of Butlin's Luxury Holiday Camps at Clacton & Skegness *Weekly 3d.*

Sir Kenneth Barnes, Principal of the Royal Academy of Dramatic Art, looked at me from over the top of his glasses and said 'What is a Redcoat, James?' 'Redcoats, Sir Kenneth', I said, 'work at Butlin's Holiday Camps. They make sure everyone is having a good time and plenty of fun.'

It was 1949. I was a drama student and had spent the summer holidays working at Pwllheli Holiday Camp as a Redcoat. I don't think dear old Sir Kenneth understood what I was talking about, but that summer I'd experienced something that I've never forgotten – to be working in an atmosphere where all one's waking hours were devoted to making sure people enjoyed themselves. They were indeed golden days at Butlin's. The war had only been over four years and rationing was still in progress and life was very hard for most of the population. People wanted to forget the long dreary years behind them and have the holiday of their lives at a modest cost, and Billy Butlin was the man who gave

it to them. He possessed that rare gift 'the common touch'. He knew what people wanted and made sure they got it.

In those days at Pwllheli there was a special railway station that came right into the camp and on Saturdays, when the new holidaymakers arrived, there would be a band and all the Redcoats waiting to greet them. As they poured out of the trains, the campers' faces were gleaming with eager anticipation and they were not disappointed. What a week it was – a never-ending feast of fun and togetherness! The variety of competitions were endless – Knobbly Knees, Holiday Princess, Ugly Face, Glamorous Grandmother, Campers' Concert – there was something for everyone. To the blasé eyes of the overfed, over-entertained 1980s this may all seem rather trivial and childish, but thirty-five years ago it was a ray of sunshine and hope in a dreary drab world.

When my partner David Croft

Right, Entertainments Manager from BBC TV series *Hi-de-Hi!*

and I first started writing *Hi-de-Hi*, it was from our rich experience working at Butlin's that we drew our inspiration. Until that time, comedy shows about holiday camps consisted mainly of jokes about barbed wire, guard dogs and stopping people from getting out. But we wrote about the things we knew and remembered, and in *Hi-de-Hi* people wanted to come in – into a magic world of fun, fun, fun.

Stories amongst performers who started their careers at Butlin's are legion and whenever we get together the memories come thick and fast.

The amount of live entertainment was amazing. Every camp had a resident revue company, two dance bands and an orchestra and not forgetting the Butlin's repertory players who performed popular plays cut down to an hour. How they managed it I'll never know. I remember watching a performance of Emlyn Williams' thriller *Night Must Fall* at a very dramatic moment in the play, the murderer Danny crept up behind the old lady in a wheelchair and raised a cushion to smother her. The audience held its breath. Suddenly a Redcoat jumped up on the side of the stage and switched on a flashing light above a board with the words 'Baby Crying' on it. Then he wrote up the number of the chalet and jumped down again. So many comics repeat this story, but in their case the number was written up just as they came to the tag of a joke.

As well as all the shows, there was the Entertainments Staff – the ballroom dancing champions who gave exhibitions nightly, the riding instructors, the camp hypnotist, the children's entertainer and Punch and Judy man and of course the camp comic who was the butt of the whole camp and was thrown into the swimming pool whenever there was a lull in the proceedings. The Redcoats joined in everything and as well as running the competitions, would always be thinking up new wheezes to keep the campers entertained and it was from all these people that David and I drew our characters for *Hi-de-Hi*.

The only one who was not taken from life was Joe Maplin. He was pure invention. In order to make the series work, we needed a villain running our camp – someone who was mean and grasping, and who exploited his staff with the fear of the sack if they stepped out of line. What a contrast to Billy Butlin, who as well as being a fine showman, was a warm generous man and a great philanthropist. The story that everyone tells about Billy Butlin is the one about the dead goldfish. They all have their own version and over the years it has been embroidered and changed to suit the mood of the raconteur. Whenever the great man inspected his camps, the first thing he did was to look in the dustbins. If a large amount of a certain dish had been thrown away, he took it off the menu. On this particular occasion, he removed the lid of one the dustbins and inside was a dead goldfish. Later that day as he was walking through the reception area with the camp manager he stopped beside a large tankful of goldfish and said to the manager 'Wait a minute, there's one missing.'

The Butlin's so many of us remember has gone forever, but *Hi-de-Hi* always brings the memories of those golden days flooding back.

Jimmy Perry
1985

HELLO CAMPERS!

Above and below, Jimmy Perry, circled, co-author of *Hi-de-Hi*, as a Redcoat. Pwllheli, 1949.

EARLY DAYS

Bill Butlin – rags to riches, from £5 to
£25,000 in fifteen years.

What the Butlin saw

When Bill Butlin arrived in Skegness in the summer of 1927 it was a typical middle class seaside town, genteel in the summer and desolate in the winter. Half the houses were holiday homes for the well-off from Nottingham and Derbyshire and the remainder were mostly seaside boarding houses.

The advantage of Skegness for Bill Butlin was that it was accessible. There was a station with a direct line from Kings Cross in London. The journey cost only two shillings and sixpence, and to encourage people to travel to the wilds of the Lincolnshire coast, the LNER (London North Eastern Railway) had commissioned John Hassall, in 1908, to design a poster, illustrating the appeal of the place. He never visited the town, the only thing that he had heard about was the biting east wind which whipped across the flat Lincolnshire landscape. 'Skegness,' he announced on the posters, 'is so bracing!'

In those days visitors to the seaside weren't greeted by the loud sounds and bright lights that they are today. There weren't rows of amusement arcades with video games or souvenir shops selling rock and kiss-me-quick hats. There was no night life of disco dancing accompanied by the smell of fried onions and hot dogs.

In the 1920s and 1930s the main focal point of the seaside was the pier, with its 'What the Butler Saw' machines, and open air concert party pierrot shows made up of acrobats and dancers. During the day a pierrot troupe performed on the beach, and members of the company went round afterwards with a collecting box for donations. If it rained the performance was cancelled.

The little wooden huts along the sea-front, opened up in the summer, selling rock and fizzy drinks. There were Punch-and-Judy shows and a tent with a little bioscope showing the first silent movies. The few holiday makers who were lucky enough to be able to afford to escape from the dull, dingey cities to the coast would promenade up and down the sea front when the sun shone, buying whelks from a stall, and when it rained, as it frequently did, they would huddle under the few shop awnings or tram shelters.

The only free entertainment for children, apart from paddling in the sea, was making sandcastles, whilst the adults dozed in hired deck chairs trying to catch the sun. Having a tan had suddenly become fashionable. They bought small china vases or leather book marks or wallets as seaside souvenirs to take home, and proudly show their friends.

Roll Up! Roll Up! All The Fun Of The Fair

There wasn't anything particularly surprising about Bill Butlin opening an amusement site – after all he came from a West Country fairground family. By the age of six he was travelling around with the fair helping his mother sell gingerbread from a caravan.

In 1921 Bill Butlin arrived back in

8

Right, Bill Butlin circled, with his uniformed staff, Skegness, 1928.

Skegness is <u>so</u> bracing!

England from Canada, with only five pounds to his name. He was twenty-one, and the first thing he did was walk from Liverpool to Bristol to find his fairground relatives. They immediately told him there was no future for him in England, and tried to persuade him to return to Canada. But he was determined to make a go of it, so his relatives agreed to help him, and he set up a hoopla stall for thirty shillings. He beat the competition by offering bigger rings, smaller pegs, and better prizes. For the next few years Bill Butlin travelled round the country with the fair, and was so successful that three years later he had stalls with Bertram Mills Christmas amusements at Olympia.

It was whilst travelling around that Bill Butlin became aware that the crowds at funfairs, along with the takings, were starting to dwindle away. It wasn't long before he discovered that people were following the latest craze: charabanc trips to the seaside. Whole villages and factories would get together and save all year to hire a charabanc for the women and children to go on a day trip to the coast. The men usually weren't included as they couldn't take the time off work and there was no such thing as paid holidays.

It was around this time that Bill Butlin met Albert Cronkshaw and Alfie Smith who both had stalls in Skegness. Bill Butlin hadn't ever heard of the place, but as he watched the two men spending quite a lot of money in a bar, he decided that if he was going to make a fortune he'd better pay Skegness a visit.

When he arrived he stood outside the station, and looking around he thought how small it was.

He peered through the rain at the cows grazing in the fields and tried to imagine what Skegness was like in the summer. As he walked down the main street, with its village shops and the occasional amusement stall, he decided that with the growth of charabanc trips and motoring, it could possibly be an ideal seaside resort for attracting holiday makers from the North of England and the Midlands.

Bill Butlin decided to give it a try, and he rented a piece of land a hundred yards long and a hundred feet deep in an overgrown area known to the locals of Skegness as the 'Jungle'. He covered the sand with wooden gratings for people to walk on and opened his amusement site with four hoopla stalls, a tower slide, which was a spiral chute which you careered down on a mat, a home-made haunted house and a small track for battery operated Custer cars.

Poster designed by John Hassall in 1908 for LNER.

Above, Custer cars, Skegness, 1931. Right, the first Butlin amusement on The Jungle, Skegness, 1928.

The only day of the week that the Butlin's amusement site closed was a Sunday. The other six days, the 30 or so employees were open ready for work at 9.00 in the morning. Bill Butlin had watched the movements of the holiday makers. He knew they had to leave their boarding houses immediately after break-fast, which was why he insisted that his amusements were open and ready for them first thing in the morning, just as they had to remain open after the pubs closed at night, because that was when people wondered around with money to spend. Even when it rained, and there was no one about, Bill Butlin still wouldn't allow his site to close down early.

Trevor Watts was a cousin of Bill Butlin, and came from a poor mining town in south Wales. Most of the men in his family worked down the mines, but Trevor was a thin sickly child who wasn't able to follow in their footsteps. When he was fourteen his uncle Bill offered him a job, and he travelled to Skegness and started working on the amusement sites. The first job he was given was painting the light bulbs bright funfair colours and hanging them round the edge of the site. He also exercised the guard dogs and took the sixpences for the Dodgem car rides. He remembers well the hustle and bustle and fun of the fair; how Bill Butlin's mother,

Bertha, looked after the takings at Bill's Mablethorpe site and his wife, Dolly, did the paper work at Skegness.

'The Name Is Butlin's – B.U.T.L.I.N.S.'

Bill Butlin's mother was very strict and insisted that all the Butlin's employees who dealt directly with the public had to look smart. They had to wear a collar and tie, and they weren't allowed to swear. These men weren't shop assistants, they were fairground workers, who were rough and tough and used to working outside in all

weathers erecting and dismantling fair ground amusements. They worked with their sleeves rolled up, and they didn't mince words. They didn't take kindly to the new rules, and they weren't very enthusiastic about having to wear a uniform. These were white jackets with blue collar and cuffs, and the letter 'B' embroidered in blue on the breast pocket. There were no side pockets so that nimble fingers couldn't slip the takings into them instead of into the till.

The Butlin's coats cost eight shillings and eleven pence each and were made by Wildmans, a local Skegness outfitters. At first Bill Butlin ordered six, all in average sizes, and asked if he could pay for them one at a time. Wildmans agreed to him having credit and gradually all the amuse-

Bumps-a-daisy

ment site employees were fitted out in white jackets and overalls in the Butlin's colours and bearing the Butlin's symbol. They were the first amusement site workers to wear a uniform.

Bill Butlin enlarged his amusement site empire beyond Skegness, till by the early 1930s he owned a chain of eight permanent amusement sites along the coast, and operated most of the attractions at several big Christmas fairs, as well as having seven amusement centres around London. By the time he was thirty-four he was earning £25,000 a year and moved out of his caravan which, it was rumoured, was silver plated and that he charged people a shilling to look inside, and he was able to buy a house for the first time.

During the winter when the seaside amusements closed down, Bill Butlin took his Dodgems and hoopla stalls to an old foundry in Bradford for a few weeks. Later on, he rented old factories and put in stalls and Dodgems. He temporarily took over disused bus garages and stables in London at Whitechapel, Brixton, Tooting, Putney, Hammersmith and Marble Arch and made them into funfairs which turned out to be very popular.

'I've Bumped Into Some Nice Acquaintances On the Dodgems'

The following Christmas, after his first season at Skegness, Bill Butlin returned with his amusements to Olympia. It was whilst he was there that he met an American manufacturer of fairground rides who told him about a brand new amusement. It was a miniature car, which steered just like an ordinary one, shaped like a little baby bath tub. It had thick buffers all round the outside edge, which made it quite safe for the drivers to bump and bang crash into one another, or they could use their driving skills and weave and dodge to avoid each other. Bill Butlin thought that these Dodgem cars, as they were called, sounded tremendous fun, and

would be a great attraction at his amusement sites. He studied the sketch that the American had drawn for him, and decided to buy a batch of the little cars, but they cost £2,000 pounds. He went back to his caravan and counted his money. He had £1,800. By borrowing the remaining £200 he was able to write to the manufacturer and place his order. A year later, at Whitsun 1928, Bill Butlin first introduced Dodgem cars on to his Skegness amusement site. Anyone who was good at driving them could have free rides all day. After only a few weeks, the excitement of banging and crashing the cars safely into one another caught on and they were a success. Over the next few months Bill Butlin acquired the sole agency for selling Dodgem cars in Europe.

The news of the thrills and the fun of the Dodgems travelled fast around the fairgrounds and it wasn't long before Bill Butlin had sold hundreds. Within the next couple of years the money he made enabled him to move his amusements from the 'Jungle' site, to a more prestigious position by Skegness pier, and also to take over another site at the end of the promenade. As well as the Dodgems he had all the old funfair favourites; the mystery cave in which were bumped and banged by skeletons and creepy-crawlies as you walked through; the distorting mirrors which made you change shape as you looked at your reflection, and the tumbling tubes, which were three huge drums all revolving in opposite ways which you had to try and walk through. There was toffee-making and people demonstrating how the letters were put into seaside rock. They sold candy floss, brandy snaps, fizzy pop, home-made ice cream, striped humbugs and white and pink nougat cut from huge blocks.

The Fasting Vicar of Stiffkey

During the late 1920s amusement sites attracted some very peculiar side shows.

Right, Bill Butlin driving a Dodgem car on his Skegness amusement site. 1930.
Inset, Duke of Kent at the Glasgow Exhibition, driving a car on the Butlin's Speedway. 1938.

Skeletons and creepy-crawlies

Some of them were very popular such as dwarfs, Siamese twins or people who were grossly overweight or underweight. One of the more unusual ones that eventually ended up on the Butlin's site at Skegness was the Vicar of Stiffkey. He had become notorious after being de-frocked for going with prostitutes and had decided to exploit his fame by taking a stall in Tottenham Court Road in London, and sitting in a barrel and fasting.

The idea caught on, and crowds paid to see the Vicar of Stiffkey wearing his dog collar, sitting up in a barrel. His stall was open twenty-four hours a day, except occasionally he would close it down for a few minutes announcing that he had to 'attend to a call of nature'. The truth was it allowed him to go and eat. The weeks passed, and it became obvious that the fasting vicar definitely wasn't wasting away, so gradually his popularity waned and the queues began to dwindle.

He decided to take his barrel to the seaside, and he chose Blackpool. He got a stall on the seafront, sat himself in his barrel and continued fasting. But again it wasn't very long before the crowds realised that there wasn't any curiosity value in paying to see him, because he wasn't getting any thinner. Eventually he was forced to find an unexploited public, and

he moved on to Skegness, where he took a stall on one of the Butlin's amusement sites.

The Vicar of Stiffkey, a shrewd business man, soon realised that fasting in a barrel had lost its appeal, and that he would have to come up with something new. He decided he would risk life and limb by sitting in a lion's cage. So he arrived in Skegness with a friendly lion called Freddy, who loved having his tummy tickled. Word soon got around about the de-frocked vicar sitting in a lion's cage, and the takings proved the idea was an immediate success.

But unfortunately the fame was short lived. The de-frocked vicar was a bad-tempered man who drank heavily and frequently hit Freddie the lion with a large stick, apparently having no respect for the fact he shared its cage. He ignored the warnings of the fairground workers who told him that Freddie wouldn't put up with it for much longer. He continued to hit the lion, until one day it simply had enough of the vicar's behaviour, and ate him.

Another strange, but not so notorious act on Bill Butlin's amusement site, was a man who played the piano non-stop day and night. But at night, when everybody went home, there was no-one to check if he stopped playing or not.

Alf was another. He was buried alive

underground in a coffin, apparently without food. There was a pipe which ran from the interior of the coffin up to the surface, to allow Alf to breath, and people paid to look down it. When the amusement site closed, in the evening and the last holiday makers had left, Alf's food was poured down the pipe. He lived on anything that was runny, and managed to stay underground in his coffin for up to two weeks at a time.

Some of the other speciality acts that were very popular were Dare Devil Peggy, who was a one-legged diver who jumped from a diving board sixty feet high into a tank of water ten feet deep, a team of trick cyclists, and a German girl who did gymnastics on top of a fifty foot pole. Bill Butlin didn't mind what the acts were, although he preferred the more spectacular, as they drew the crowds.

The Biggest Pig In The World

One of the Butlin's amusements sites was at Felixstowe, where a man called Joe Gardner had a franchise on a stall and exhibited the 'Biggest Pig' in the world. In fact it was just an ordinary sized pig, but it was made to appear huge by being stood in a tiny pen on a raised platform which was hidden with straw. This trickery made the pig look as if it was the size of a baby elephant. One day a West Country farmer told Joe that he had a bigger pig. Joe went and looked at it, and it was bigger, so he bought the competition for £20. When the novelty of the biggest pig in the world wore off, Joe introduced a new side show, which was 'The Smallest Horse in the World'. But again this was just trickery. The horse was a Shetland pony that had been shaved and stood it in the middle of a huge pen. Instead of raising it up on a platform, as he'd done with the pig, he stood the horse in a hollow, which made it look as if it was the size of a whippet. The smallest pony was as popular to the seaside crowds as the biggest pig had been.

But the public were fickle, and quickly got bored. Joe decided to introduce yet another phenomena, which was the 'Only Pigmy Princess In Captivity'. She was in fact an African midget, who wore a grass skirt and bangles. Like the pig and the pony before her, she was stood in the middle of a huge pen in a hollow in the ground to make her successfully appear even smaller than she really was. She drew in the crowds, and the takings. Joe was doing well until a man from the Colonial Office arrived on the site and asked to see her immigration papers. Unfortunately she didn't have any, and neither did Joe, so she was sent home.

Roundabout Butlin's
The 1890's roundabout at Skegness was originally called Whites Zoological Roundabout, the rides were ostriches, cockerels and horses. It is the only one with 56 galloping animals four abreast in sets of 14. Bill Butlin bought it from Barry Island in the 1930's for Skegness. Fibreglass horses replaced the old animals.

Canvas City

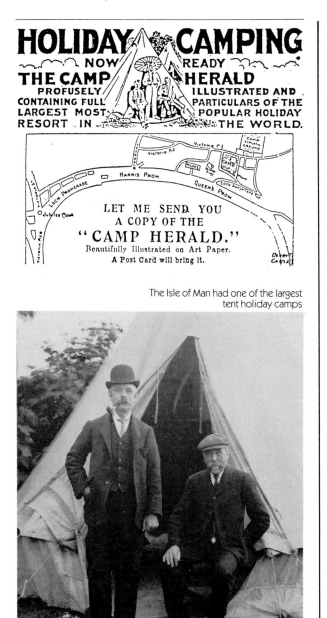

HOLIDAY CAMPING

NOW READY

THE CAMP HERALD

PROFUSELY ILLUSTRATED AND CONTAINING FULL PARTICULARS OF THE LARGEST MOST POPULAR HOLIDAY RESORT IN THE WORLD.

LET ME SEND YOU A COPY OF THE "CAMP HERALD." Beautifully Illustrated on Art Paper. A Post Card will bring it.

The Isle of Man had one of the largest tent holiday camps

In the winter of 1935 Bill Butlin's cousin, Trevor Watts, was working at Olympia looking after his uncle's amusements. On Boxing Day Bill paid Trevor a visit and asked him if he'd like to go back to working at the seaside. Trevor was surprised by the suggestion because all the coastal amusement sites were closed for the winter. But Bill Butlin had a new venture in mind. He wanted Trevor to go and help a Captain Harry Warner build a holiday camp at Seaton in Devon. Captain Warner already had a small holiday camp at Dover Court, in Sussex, where Bill Butlin had an amusement site, and the two men had met through doing a deal over some Dodgem cars.

Bill Butlin had experienced holiday camps before the First World War, when he was a young boy working for Eatons departmental store in Toronto, Canada. He had stayed at the Eatons holiday camp which provided accommodation on the shores of Lake Ontario. It was one of his happiest childhood memories, and he never forgot the sing-songs, the get-togethers, and the organised fun and games.

Holiday camps weren't a new idea in England. In the 1920s there were quite a few of them dotted about the countryside. The first one to be run along modern lines and to cater for families was Dodd's Socialist Holiday Camp in Caister, which opened in 1906. But two of the most famous were Mother Garibaldi's, at Great Yarmouth, and Cunningham's Young Men's Holiday Camp on the Isle of Wight, which had 60,000 visitors a year.

Cunningham's offered its campers team games, sing-songs and other organised amusements, as well as a heated swimming pool, a valet service, barber's shop, vast dining and concert halls and a bank. But there were drawbacks. Every camper had to sign a pledge on their booking form promising that they would not touch alcohol or use improper language. No

women were allowed to stay on the camp and the sleeping accommodation consisted of rows and rows of candle-lit tents. Cunningham's wasn't aimed at families, but it was a very popular holiday place for robust outdoor young men.

When Bill Butlin started thinking about going into the holiday camp business, he paid Cunningham's a visit. He wandered around and listened to the campers singing 'Auld Lang Syne' the evening before they left. He noticed the little metal badges that each camper paid one penny for and wore in order to recognise one another when they were off the site. He watched the team games and sing-songs. But when he asked the Cunningham family if he could take a look at the kitchens, they refused. Because there was no such thing as convenience foods then, there had to be an army of chefs, kitchen staff and gadgets to be able to cater for such large numbers of people. The Cunningham family

couldn't stop Bill Butlin from wandering around the camp site, but they could stop him from seeing how they dealt with mass catering, with their specially designed dishwasher that could wash 20,000 plates after every meal and their automatic potato and bread slicers, which were all powered by steam. Most of the food was prepared in vast pressure cookers. Although Bill Butlin didn't see the kitchens, he saw enough to get the general idea.

'Oh! I Do Love To Be Beside The Seaside'

The seaside didn't provide entertainment when the weather was bad, and the seaside landladies only allowed their guests back inside as long as they sat in silence. To most holiday makers, especially those with children which were impossible to keep still and quiet, it was preferable to stay out and shelter from the rain.

Staying in a seaside boarding house

THE CUNNINGHAM CAMP. DOUGLAS.   38

Hurrah! It's Butlin's!

meant sleeping in a small clean room with a wash stand in it. A jug of hot water was brought in the morning and another at night, with the proviso that the wallpaper mustn't be splashed. The lavatory was shared by everyone and there was usually no bath. Bread and jam were served for breakfast, except on Sundays, when there was something cooked. At tea-time there was a hot meal, which was served quickly and eaten in silence. In those days there was no radio and no television. Once it was dark, it was time for bed.

Bill Butlin had once stayed in a cheap boarding house in Barry, in North Wales. He had experienced the misery of being thrown out straight after breakfast by the landlady, and regardless of the weather, not allowed back in until either lunch or tea-time. He watched families with small children, huddled in tram shelters from the predictable rain of an English summer, with nowhere to go.

In the larger seaside towns there were dance halls and maybe an outdoor pierrot show in the evening, if it wasn't rained off. But these activities were not for people with children. Families weren't catered for, so they usually only went to the seaside for a day trip.

Despite the few facilities, the seaside was still a place to dream about. It was wonderful for workers to get away from the big city, the grimey back-to-back houses, the daily factory and office routine, the grey industrial street and factory chimneys. A trip to the seaside by car, charabanc or train, was a high point of the year, saved for, and looked forward to with excitement matched only by the trip to the Christmas pantomime. Although holidays were still only for the privileged few who could afford to take the time off work, the idea of paid holidays was becoming more popular, and pressure was being applied on the government to make them law. The result would mean that an annual summer holiday wouldn't just be something for the well-off, but also for the ordinary factory and shop worker.

When It's Wet, It's Fine At Butlin's

It took three months to build the Warner's Holiday Camp, which opened in Easter 1935 for 200 people. Bill Butlin was on the board of the Warner's company, so it wasn't surprising that he dropped by and made a note that the chalets and dining halls were made from timber and that there were no amusements. The fifty men who helped to build the Warner's camp formed the nucleus of the team who a few months later were to build the Butlin's camp. After all, they had the experience. It was on one of his visits to the Warner's camp site that Bill Butlin told Trevor Watts that he had plans to build his own holiday camp, and it was going to be bigger and better than anything else. It would be open to men and women, as well as catering for families. There would be guaranteed entertainment, despite the unpredictable English weather, and bars, dining halls and theatres. No one would sleep in canvas tents, they would all have their own chalets.

The Fun Of A Camp, The Luxury Of A Hotel

A few months later, whilst driving from Skegness to his amusement site a few miles away in Mablethorpe, Bill Butlin stopped just before the sleepy little village of Ingoldmells to stretch his legs. He decided that the turnip field by the side of the road on which he was standing was the perfect site to build his first holiday camp.

He paid a £100 an acre, which was more than the land was worth, but he wanted all 40 acres, from the edge of Skegness right up to the sand dunes. When the locals heard of Bill Butlin's plans, they couldn't image what his holiday camp was going to look like. There wasn't anything to compare it with. Three hundred men were taken off the Butlin amusement sites to help build the camp. But that wasn't enough, and Bill Butlin had to go out into the street and ask any man who was passing whether he had a hammer and a saw – if so he would offer him a job.

—THE CAMPS — 1936: SKEGNESS—

**Holiday camps under canvas give way to
holiday camps under concrete**

The first Butlin's holiday camp opened at Skegness on Easter Saturday 1936. There was no official ceremony performed by local dignitaries, whilst marching bands played and celebrities signed autographs. There wasn't a hint of razzamatazz, or a Redcoat shouting 'Hi-De-Hi'. Instead there was a half-built camp, with a lot of unfinished buildings covered in a fine layer of snow. To make matters worse, there was no heating in the chalets. There was no hot water, and no extra blankets. After all, who would have thought that Bill Butlin's guarantee of a holiday, whatever the weather, would have been shattered by a white Easter.

One of the first campers at Skegness on that cold Easter holiday remembers taking the bed linen off the empty second bed in his chalet to try and keep warm. The new campers danced in their heavy overcoats, but it didn't seem to

Join the Butlin Buddies!

bother them. They waltzed away to a little local three-piece band, maybe to keep warm, or maybe to have the good time that they had been promised in the advertisements. The cold certainly didn't bother Mr Dutton who won 12 bottles of local beer in the Spot Prize dancing competition. He shared them with the other campers who had all contributed some money towards the prizes.

The immediate problem was the cold weather, but previously it had been finding a water supply. Despite the endless drilling that had gone on all over the Skegness camp site, they had failed to find any. The building and the drilling for water had started the previous October, but as Easter 1936 drew closer and the bore holes grew deeper, they still hadn't found any.

> **'Come on all you scholars now, and put away your studies, come and join the happy band, known as Butlin's Buddies'**

In the spring of 1936, the Butlin's camp was half built, and already it was over-booked. It had cost £50,000 and it would be even more by the time it was finished. Bill Butlin was in debt, although he knew that once the camp opened and the holiday makers paid their week's balance, the money would come pouring in. He had to convince his creditors that it was a success, or they could close down the camp, before it had even opened. He decided to impress them, and scraped together enough money to buy a Rolls Royce on hire purchase. Bill Butlin drove round Skegness in it, assuring his creditors that they would all be paid. They took one look at the opulent vehicle, and believed him. He also repainted his two dilapidated Austin Seven vans, which he used for running errands between Skegness and the camp site. He painted them bright fairground colours, and put a number 2 on the side of one, and a number 9 on the side of the other, to give the impression that they were just two of a fleet.

At a cost of £500, Bill Butlin had taken a half page advertisement in the *Daily Express* newspaper offering holidays at his camp for thirty five shillings to £3, for a week, depending on the time of the season. The price included four meals a day plus free entertainment. Within days, there were 10,000 enquiries, as well as bookings accompanied by a ten shilling deposit. The Butlin office staff of four were totally unprepared for such a response, and had to work all through the night, sending out brochures.

The Luxury of Running Water in Every Chalet!

Meanwhile, back at the camp site, the search for water was becoming even more urgent. Since the advertisement had appeared, 500 campers were expected that Easter. Men were taken off building work so that every effort could be channelled into digging bore holes. By Easter Saturday the only water that had been found on the site was a nasty blackish colour. It was all right for washing up and for baths, it would do for flushing toilets and cleaning, but it wasn't any use for drinking or cooking.

Bill Butlin could see his dream holiday camp closing before it had even opened, leaving him with a lot of creditors. In desperation he went to Skegness council and asked if he could use their water supply. Luckily for him, they agreed, and every night three Austin Seven vans loaded with milk churns shuttled backwards and forwards between Bill Butlin's house and the camp. They were filled with water from every available tap. But after only a few weeks the council decided that the demand for water from the camp was too much for their existing supply and would have to stop. If that happened the camp would have to close.

Suddenly, three weeks after Butlin's at Skegness had opened, Norman Bradford,

Bill Butlin insisted that the flags outside every site had to be flying at 10 am every morning and be down by dusk.

'In 1939 we didn't have hot water at home, we had to boil a kettle for a bath. At Butlin's there was hot water out of a tap and you could have a bath every day'

who was in charge of maintenance, brought Bill Butlin the news he so desperately needed; 400 feet down one of the many bore holes, they had found water. Bill Butlin got up earlier than usual the following day. He was so excited that he rushed round the camp feverishly turning on every tap and flushing every lavatory. The running water was the best thing he'd seen that side of the Lincolnshire coast.

Freda Monk from Nottingham was the first Butlin's camper. She arrived a day early, and was found by the manager wandering round the unfinished camp site, clutching her suitcase, looking lost. In the mad frenzy to find water, nobody had expected the arrival of an early camper. She was given food and a chalet, and like the other campers who arrived the following day, she ate her breakfast wearing an overcoat to keep out the cold. There weren't as many campers as had been expected, because one party accidently went to Sheerness, instead of Skegness.

Regardless of the new campers playing table tennis, the building continued round them. The camp swimming pool wasn't ready, there were no badges, no Redcoats and no organised sing-songs. Six people shared a dining table and the meals were reported as not being very hot and consisting of a lot of butter beans.

At one of the mealtimes the manager stood on a chair and proudly announced to the shivering campers, that despite the problems, he was pleased to be able to tell them that half of them had booked to come again!

Butlin's Luxury Holiday Camp, Skegness, c

'Our True Intent Is All for Your Delight'

The main reception was at the front of the camp site, behind the fountains and the swimming pool. It was an impressive looking building with a clock tower above it, easily seen from the road. Across the front of this building was a huge illuminated sign, which attracted the attention of passers by with the words 'Our True Intent Is All For Your Delight'. This is a quote from Shakespeare's play *A Midsummer Night's Dream*. But Bill Butlin didn't know that. He'd hardly ever been to school, let alone read plays by Shakespeare. He had seen the quote on the front of a fairground organ many years before, and had liked it so much that he had remembered it and decided to put it on the front of his new holiday camp.

the ocean and occupying an area of over 100 acres

Above and overleaf, reproduction of an early Butlin's holiday brochure in 1939 showing a standard of luxury equal to the transatlantic liners of the day.

Foreword

The thought behind the issue of this souvenir is to provide a happy ending to a perfect holiday. First there was the thrill of holiday planning, then the holiday itself. Now comes the pleasure of looking back through these pages, which, it is hoped, will help you to live again the happy carefree days you spent with us.

A view of the Camp from the Sea

Furnished Bungalows by the sea set in spacious lawns and beautiful gardens

The Hawaiian Lounge in Gloucester House

The Empress Ball Room in a realistic Viennese setting

and outdoor sport. Bowls for those who prefer a milder competition

The Dungeon Bar
at The Pig and Whistle

One of the star attractions—the largest heated open-air Swimming Pool on the East Coast.

Luxuriously designed dining halls

The late Duke and Duchess of Gloucester and Mr. Butlin after the opening ceremony of the new Gloucester House

And now—The last word in American Cocktail Bars

Plenty of indoor fun—

One of the Sun Lounges for the restful hour

Some of our famous Guest Stars—Gracie Fields, Elsie and Doris Waters, Will Fyffe, Tommy Trinder, Len Harvey, Jack Doyle, Harricani and his Tipica Orchestra—here often and by Royal

Faith, Hope, and Chalet Key

Roses painted between chalets

The Butlin's Elizabethan Chalet

The Butlin's camp was built to accommodate a thousand holiday makers, in 600 chalets, which like all the other buildings were designed by Bill Butlin. He drew the plans on the back of a cigarette packet. Each chalet was going to cost about £10 to build, and would be ten foot by ten foot in size, standing in its own 'grounds' surrounded by flower borders.

Each one would have its own electricity and cold running water and, because Bill Butlin believed that people went on holiday to escape from their drab surroundings and grey buildings, the exterior walls would be painted different colours; pastel pink, blue or yellow. The idea was that chalets would be basic but homely. There would be curtains at the windows, made from fabric with little yachts printed on it, and inside the camper would find a three-sided wooden cupboard made from match-boxing fixed to the wall, with a curtain across the front, where they could hang their clothes. The bed would have blue candlewick cover, with the already famous letter 'B' embroidered on it, as well as on the pink and blue sheets and blankets. On the floor there was a small rug covering the varnished wooden boards. There was a wash basin, with only one tap for cold water, and next to it a square hole where another could be fitted, a forty watt light bulb, and a small mirror, with a notice next to it forbidding the use of stoves or spirit lamps. At the end of each line of chalets there was a block of about twenty baths, which had both hot and cold running water, and lavatories, which were labelled 'Lads' and 'Lassies'.

Construction:
timber framed, infilled
with chicken wire
covered with cement

Interior sprung mattress
upholstered with
curled black hair
designed to support
the back for correct
sleeping position

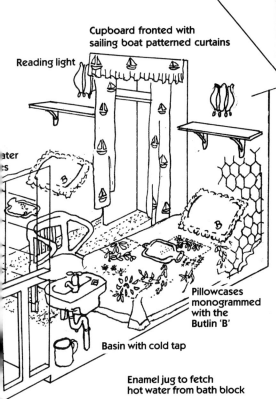

Cupboard fronted with
sailing boat patterned curtains

Reading light

ater
es

Pillowcases
monogrammed
with the
Butlin 'B'

Basin with cold tap

Enamel jug to fetch
hot water from bath block

Where will my Teddy sleep tonight?

Six weeks after the Skegness camp opened Ron Blow and two of his friends arrived for their first ever holiday by the sea. They hadn't ever been able to afford one before, and although the cost of Butlin's was about the same price as staying at a boarding house, the entertainment was free. The first thing that struck them when they arrived was the size of the place, they thought it was huge and beautiful, and they weren't at all bothered by the number of unfinished buildings.

They were put in chalet G4 which they thought was very nice, with its two little single beds and space for a suitcase underneath each one. They didn't bother to unpack, they were so excited that they went off to explore the camp site. The first people that Ron and his friends met were two girls in tears. After trying to comfort them, they discovered that the girls had arrived at lunchtime and found that their chalet had only three walls, no roof, no door, and no furniture.

Ron and his friends felt sorry for them, and offered them their chalet. When they returned three hours later, they were very surprised to find the girls chalet had a roof, door, electric light and curtains at the windows.

There was a temporary reception area, with rows of card tables and buckets of keys, one key fitted all the chalet locks. Campers were handing over cash and the tables were covered ,with piles of pound notes. After a couple of months the buildings were finished.

Bong, Bong, Radio Keep Fit Calling

Along the chalet lines, positioned every few hundred yards, there were tall poles with loud speakers on the top. There were hundreds of them dotted all over the camp, and these speakers were used to give out the early morning 'Wakey, Wakey' calls, telling the campers that it was a beautiful day and breakfast was going to be served in half an hour. All day the

BUTLIN'S SKEGNESS HOLIDAY CAMP.

1442

1459

Tannoy loudspeaker system broadcast announcements about the morning Keep Fit with Cappy Bond and various sports activities, meal time reminders, the whereabouts of a lost child and SOS messages or telegrams. It would also relay to the campers any important items picked up on the BBC. Radio Butlin was run, like most of the entertainment activities on the camp, by the Redcoats.

So you wanna be a Star?

Hustle Bustle

That first season the camp was so over-subscribed that Bill Butlin took a whole page advertisement in the local newspaper announcing that he had too many bookings, and if the landladies of Skegness contacted his office, he would happily give them the names and address of the holidaymakers he wasn't able to accommodate.

The locals of Skegness had been very wary at first about Butlin's holiday camp. They thought it was going to take away their livelihood, and ruin their town, so they refused to allow it to be built within their boundaries. But they soon found that Butlin's brought a lot of business to the area, and not just from holidaymakers. The camp bought its vast supplies of food from the local butchers and farmers, and companies like the Skegness steam laundry, which cleaned all the thousands of sheets and pillow cases every week, were just one of many who serviced the camp.

All the Butlin's maintenance kitchen and cleaning staff, an enormous army of people, lived locally, and when the campers started coming into the town spending their money, Skegness started to change from being a genteel seaside town, to a hustling, bustling holiday resort.

Hollywood At Butlin's

One morning Annie Watson was swimming in the pool, when a man who had been watching her for some time, told her that he was using the camp to make a feature film. It was called 'Sam Small Leaves Town', and starred Stanley Holloway, June Clyde and James Craven. He was Alfred Goulding, the director, and he asked Annie if she would like to be in it, as he needed someone who was good at diving from the high board. She was so excited that she agreed immediately. After filming several scenes diving into the pool, the director said that if Annie had a long

evening dress, he would like her to be in the dancing sequences. She had bought several long evening dresses with her, and so along with some other campers Annie went filming in the ballroom.

The filming started at midnight after the majority of campers, and Annie's husband, had gone to bed. For the following four nights they worked until three in the morning. Annie, wearing her long blue satin evening dress, walked into the dining room behind June Clyde and James Craven. But on the fourth night Annie was exhausted from lack of sleep, and finally her husband refused to allow her to do any more. She was given a blue leather handbag as payment for her hard work.

Left, Stanley Holloway, star of 'Sam Small Leaves Town'. Above, marked with a cross, and below on the diving board, Bathing Beauty Annie Watson

88 c 38

BUTLINS SKEGNESS HOLIDAY CAMP

1652

Come and join our happy gang

Lights out campers

Norman Bradford and another Redcoat, Frank Cusworth, both had the job of entertaining campers in the bars. When it was time to close they found it very difficult to get them to drink up and leave. Nobody wanted to spoil the holiday atmosphere, but there had to be a closing time.

A film called *Chain Gang* was on the cinema circuit at the time, and one evening just for fun, when it was time for the bar to close, Norman put his hands on Frank's shoulders, just as he'd seen the chain gang workers do in the film, and they shuffled across the floor towards the door. The campers joined them, until eventually they had a long chain of people, all with their hands on each other's shoulders, snaking their way round the tables and chairs. They went from the bar to the ballroom, and the line grew longer and the bars emptier.

The next day Frank decided that this could be a very successful way of clearing people out of the bars and ballrooms. The only thing that was missing was a song to liven it up, so 'Penny on the Drum' was written in the style of the Salvation Army song, 'Come and Join Us'. It exhausted and sobered up the campers ready for bed.

TWO BUTLIN SONGS FOR THE BUTLIN BUDDIES

We on-ly want a tan-ner, To buy a new pi-

a - no, So please put a penny on the drum.

Come and join us, come and join

us, Come and join our hap-py gang,

Come and join us, come and join

us, Come and join our hap-py throng.

1.

2.

Will you throng.

opening. It could accommodate 5,400, and was closed in 1983.

Holidays with play, the Clacton way

Happy Christmas At Clacton

The Butlin's camp at Clacton opened for Christmas 1938. There was no heating in any of the buildings and everyone complained about the cold. Bill Butlin found a solution, he bought some metal dustbins, and made them look like braziers by making holes round the bottom, with a red light bulb inside, surrounded by small balls of screwed-up paper. They were then put round the dining halls and ballrooms, and everyone said they felt much warmer.

Clacton – Holidays With Pay, Holidays With Play

In the late 1930s only about three million people in Britain had paid holidays. Bill Butlin's holiday camp at Skegness, enlarged to take 5000 campers, had certainly caught on. Bill Butlin was so confident that paid holidays would become law, that in 1938 he opened a second camp on the east coast, next to his amusement site at Clacton.

The layout and look of the Clacton camp were identical to Skegness. The chalets were built to the same design and from the same material, and the campers name was printed on a little card stuck on the door. The camp was divided into the same houses. There were Redcoats to organise the games and competitions and to gee-up the campers with the same, already famous 'Hi-De-Hi'. On every camper's dining table there was a pencil, a hand mirror and a programme of the day's events. In the evening a waiter in full

evening dress walked amongst the tables with a serviette over one arm, asking people what they wanted to drink. There was a quiet lounge full of comfortable armchairs where campers could sit with the morning papers and coffee. Clacton camp was soon as successful as Skegness.

That same year, 1938, the Parliamentary Bill for all industrial workers to have a week's paid holiday became law. In those days the average weekly wage was three pounds ten shillings and Bill Butlin advertised his camps with the slogan; 'A Week's Holiday For A Week's Pay', plus all the entertainment was free. The new law was just what Bill Butlin had been waiting for. It was obviously going to increase the popularity of his camps.

Summer Lasts Longer At Butlin's

Early in the summer of 1939 Bill Butlin wanted to expand and looked for another site to build a camp. He chose a 400 acres at Filey in Yorkshire. That same year nearly 100,000 people were on holiday at Butlin's Skegness and Clacton camps. Bill Butlin refused to believe the rumours that were circulating about war being imminent, although the Tannoy system at Clacton and Skegness were continually interrupting their entertainment broadcasts to give names of men who had to report back to their home town for call-up.

Reservists, school teachers and air raid wardens were all told to cancel their holidays, and by the end of August the numbers of people on the two camps had been reduced to only 6,000. The first weekend of September Bill Butlin left Clacton camp, and returned to Skegness, after reassuring holiday makers that there wasn't going to be a war. The Butlin's Times carried the headline:

'Bye-Bye Blues At BUTLIN'S?
Campers forget the crisis. Are
we downhearted? No!!'

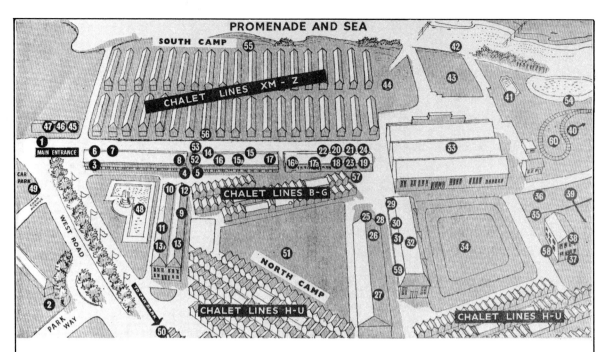

YOUR HOLIDAY PLAN of CLACTON CAMP

1 Main Entrance
2 Garage and Cycle Hire

Swimming Pool Building
Gd. Floor
3 South Seas Bar and Coffee Lounge
4 Photographic Shop and Gents' Outfitters
5 Hairdresser's Shop
52 Ice Cream Shop
53 Fruit Shop

Swimming Pool Building
1st Floor
6 Rock 'n' Calypso Ballroom
7 Indoor Swimming Pool
8 Card Room Lounge

Reception Building
9 Reception and Coffee Bar
10 Lounge Bar and Playhouse Theatre
11 Reception and Campers' Mail Office
12 Western Bar
13 Bowling Green – Upstairs
13A Dining Room

Regency Building
14 Regency Ballroom – Upstairs
15 Regency Bar – Upstairs
15A Shops – Ground Floor
16 TV Rooms
16B Chinese Restaurant

Double-decker Building
Gd. Floor
17 Fish Restaurant – Upstairs
17A Regency Cafe
18 Pig and Whistle Bar
19 Shops
20 Bendix Launderette
21 Ironing Room

Double-decker Building
1st Floor
22 Games Room
23 Ice Cream and Soda Fountain
24 Amusement Arcade
25 Foyer Coffee Bar
26 Gaiety Theatre
27 Stadium
28 Shopping Arcade Entrance

29 Newsagents
30 Radio Butlin
31 Post Office
32 Viennese Ballroom
33 Dining Hall
34 Sports Field
35 Infants' Playground
36 Skating Rink
37 Infants' Services (Ground Floor)
38 Beaver Room (First Floor)
39 Sports Field and Tennis Courts
40 Putting Green
41 Yachting Pond
42 Deck Chairs
43 Gardens
44 Children's Playground
45 British Railways' office
46 Camp Chapel
47 Medical Services
48 Outdoor Swimming Pool
49 Car Park opposite Camp
50 Car Park on Camp
51 Children's Amusement Park
54 Boating Lake
55 Sun Terrace
56 & 57 Chalet Offices
58 Pram Hire
59 Drug Store
60 Miniature Railway

When Skegness camp had opened, two years previously, there had been no official ceremony and as the first campers arrived Bill Butlin was still busy trying to find water and get the roofs on the chalets. But when Clacton Camp opened, he hired a special train to bring a party of 200 VIPs from London, and he invited every Member of Parliament who had supported the paid holidays Bill. Lord Strabolgi performed the official opening ceremony and the place was overrun by the press.

Happy days are jolly days

10,000 campers stayed at the Butlin's camps at Skegness and Clacton. Every day they ate their way through four tons of potatoes, and slept on 9,000 sheets. They used 88,250 blankets, enough to cover 55 football pitches, and one year 9,467 cups were broken. The swimming pool needed 67,000 gallons of chlorinated water and one an a half tons of powder crystal were used to grind into the ballroom floor. 400 lengths of chalk marked the sports scores, and Butlin's supplied 48,000 forks and spoons, alot of which were taken home as souvenirs.

SATURDAY
May 10th, 1947

9.30 a.m.	**Fun and Games** in the Regency Ballroom.
10.00 a.m.	**"Bingo"** in the Regency Ballroom.
2.30–3.15 p.m.	**Skating Rink Hockey Match.**
2.30–3.15 p.m.	**Afternoon Music** presented by the Butlin Concert Orchestra, directed by Al Freid. In the Regency Ballroom.
3.00–5.30 p.m.	Non-stop organ recital by George Carr, at the Hammond Organ. In the Theatre.
3.15 p.m.	**"Keep Fit in Rhythm"** with the famous **Butlin Eight.** On the Skating Rink.
3.30 p.m.	**The Nine Avalons,** world famous skating team, on the Skating Rink.
4.00 p.m.	**"Dare Devil Peggy"** in his sensational high diving act. And a demonstration by the Frogman. At the Pool.
4.00–5.30 p.m.	**Tea Dance and Floor Show,** with Dick Denny and his Dance Orchestra in the Regency Ballroom.
5.00 p.m.	**Skating Rink Hockey Match.**
5.00 p.m.	**"Keep Fit in Rhythm".** The Butlin Eight present their floor show. In the Regency Ballroom.
5.30 p.m.	**Conducted Tour of the Camp.** Meet your House Captain in the Regency Ballroom.
6.30 p.m.	**London International Orchestra** conducted by **Fistoulari. Soloist – Solomon.** In the Viennese Ballroom. (Admission by Ticket only)..
7.30–8.30 p.m.	Meet the Redcoats! **"Who's Who"** and **"Butlin Follies of 1947".** With the Butlin Concert Orchestra under the direction of Al Freid in the Theatre.
8.45–11.15 p.m.	Grand **"Get Together Dance"** and **Floor Show** with Dick Denny and his Dance Orchestra. In the Regency Ballroom.
10.30 p.m.	**Penny-on-the-Drum.** In the Regency Bar.
10.45 p.m.	**The Nine Avalons** present their sensational **Floor Show** in the Regency Ballroom.
11.15 p.m.	**Goodnight Campers.**

TUESDAY
May 13th, 1947

9.45–10.30 a.m.	**Fun and Games** with Morry Morris.
10.45–12 noon	**"Bingo"** in the Regency Ballroom.
12 noon–12.30 p.m.	Boxing Practise in the Theatre.
2.00–2.30 p.m.	Organ Recital in the Theatre, relayed to the Regency Ballroom.
2.30 p.m.	**Billiards and Snooker.** Competitions for the Lads. **Miniature Bowls** for the Lasses. In the Billiards Hall.
2.30–4.00 p.m.	**"Music on Vacation"** presented by the Butlin Concert Orchestra under the direction of Al Freid. In the Regency Ballroom.
0–5.30 p.m.	**Treasure Hunt** Assemble in the Regency Ballroom.
7.30–8.30 p.m.	**Boxing** in the Theatre by the Hull City Police Club. With a demonstration of **Keep Fit in Rhythm** by the famous **Butlin Eight.**
8.45–11.15 p.m.	**Old-Time Dancing** to the Music of Al Freid and the Butlin Concert Orchestra. In the Regency Ballroom.
11.15 p.m.	Goodnight Campers.

FRIDAY
May 16th, 1947

9.45–10.30 a.m.	**Your Last Day with Morry Morris** in the Regency Ballroom.
10.45–12 noon	**"Bingo"** in the Regency Ballroom.
12 noon–12.30 p.m.	Organ Recital in the Theatre.
2.00–2.30 p.m.	Organ Recital in the Theatre, relayed to the Regency Ballroom.
2.30–4.00 p.m.	**Afternoon Music** presented by the Butlin Concert Orchestra directed by Al Freid. In the Regency Ballroom.
4.00–5.30 p.m.	**Tea Dance and Floor Show** with Dick Denny and his Dance Orchestra. In the Regency Ballroom.
4.15 p.m.	**Whist Drive** in the Card Room.
5.00 p.m.	**The Brandy Trio** Present their Floor Show in the Regency Ballroom.
7.30–8.30 p.m.	**Dick Denny's Guest Night.** In the Theatre.
9.00–11.15 p.m.	**Au Revoir Dance and Floor Show** with Dick Denny and his Dance Orchestra. In the Regency Ballroom.
10.35 p.m.	**Prince Zahoor.** Indian Bamboo Pole Acrobat. In the Regency Ballroom.
11.00 p.m.	The Redcoats say **"Au Revoir"** to departing Campers. Goodnight Campers and Auld Land Syne.

BUTLIN'S AT WAR, 'ARE WE DOWNHEARTED?' 'NO'

'Will Re-Open When Finished With Hitler'

When war was declared on September 3rd, the lights went out all over the Butlin's camps, and a great cheer went up from the campers because they were young and mostly single and excited at the prospect of being left in the dark! The comedian, Izzy Bonn topped the bill at the Sunday night camp concert, the next day Skegness camp was taken over by the Royal Navy. Butlin's workers went round Skegness pasting over advertisements for the camp, a sign which read, 'Will re-open when finished with Hitler'. Most of the campers hurriedly began packing their cases.

That weekend Admiral Buckley walked into Bill Butlin's office on the camp site and asked him how quickly he could clear the place. The campers were gone in twenty-four hours, they were either given their money back, or a voucher to finish their holiday after the war. People who had booked and paid a deposit in advance, received a letter telling them the camp was closed, but they could have their holiday the moment it re-opened. The winners of a Gaumont Cinema competition, who had won a week's free holiday at Butlin's, were due to arrive the weekend war was declared. They were immediately sent a telegram telling them they could have their prize holiday when the war was over. Bill

Butlin never doubted his camps would re-open, despite the fact that the windows of the chalets and the dining halls were being blacked out whilst the last holiday makers were still there. The Redcoats piled their jackets in a stock room and locked them away. Butlin's Skegness camp was about to become a ship.

'Spud Bashing In The Pig & Whistle'

The Butlin's camp at Clacton was transferred from the Air Force to the Army, and in 1939 became an internment camp for German civilians. Chalets were knocked down to allow a straight perimeter wire to be put up, with floodlights every few hundred yards. But there were so few internees that it wasn't long before the camp was taken over by the Pioneer Corps.

Just as they had done at Skegness, the buildings were quickly adapted for their new role. Bren guns were repaired in the ballroom, the tennis courts became the parade ground, and commandos in full kit did their training in the swimming pool. Spud bashing was in the Pig & Whistle bar.

Right, a 1939 picture magazine, *Illustrated*.

Below left, Butlin's Home Guard practice drill with wooden rifles.

Below, expecting a short war, staff post 100,000 Christmas cards in December 1939 to let campers know that Butlin's will still be there when we've won.

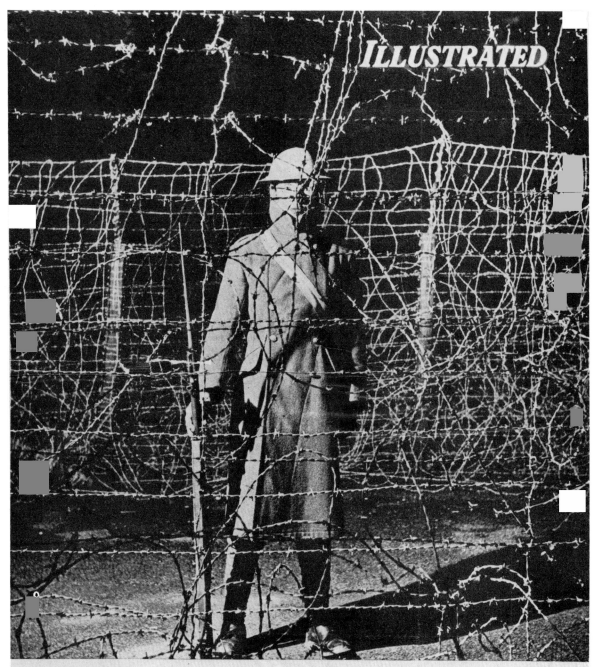

Between double rows of barbed wire fencing, the sentry stands on duty at the internment camp where German civilians now live. Guards at intervals of fifteen yards keep watch night and day, ready for any eventuality, and gone is the carefree atmosphere of what, a few weeks ago, was a holiday camp. But, says the Commandant—

"Gentlemen . . .

in this internment camp you will not be bullied. I hope we shall be good friends. You will not suffer any unnecessary discomfort. Our code is framed for your happiness"

41

(continued overleaf)

Jolly Jack Tars

'Roll up, roll up, 'nock 'itler's 'ead 'orf'

During the first few months of the war, all the rides on the Butlin's seaside amusement sites were packed away. At Bognor, the small side-show stalls were left standing but locked up. One of them was a shooting range which had the heads of the Nazi leaders; Hitler, Goering, Goebels and Ribbentrop as targets. Only after Dunkirk, and with talk of a German invasion, did Bill Butlin have the faces painted out.

With everything closed down, Walter Hilton, who was in charge of the camp bars and shops, took the accounts for the amusement sites and the holiday camps to the Butlin's head office in Oxford Street, for safe keeping.

No-one Loses at Butlin's

At the time war was declared, Bill Butlin was one of the few people who had any experience in mass catering, and who already had buildings that could hold thousands of people. The government were desperately looking for somewhere that could cheaply and quickly be adapted for large numbers of servicemen. It was decided that the Butlin's camps at Clacton and Skegness fitted the bill perfectly. For the use of both of them the Government agreed to pay Bill Butlin a rent of 25% of the previous year's profits. Within a matter of days, the Navy had taken over the camp at Skegness and the Army had taken over the one at Clacton.

It was costing the Army £125 a head to build a camp. Bill Butlin said he could build one for £75 a head. The £50 saving on each of the many thousands of heads amounted to a great deal of money, and Bill Butlin agreed to pay anything over his quote.

The deal that was that the camps would be used to house servicemen, and at the end of the war Bill Butlin could buy them back at three-fifths of their original cost, whatever condition they were in.

Bill Butlin had started to build a camp at Filey. Hore-Belisha, the War Minister, told him to finish it and the government would pay the cost. He also asked Bill Butlin to

THE "DECK" OF H.M.S. ROYAL ARTHUR, A HOLIDAY CAMP WHICH THE ADMIRALTY HAS TAKEN OVER

THESE MEN, MARCHING PAST THE COMMODORE, HAVE ONLY BEEN IN THE SERVICE A FEW WEEKS

FLASHING A MESSAGE DURING TRAINING IN SIGNALLING

All Aboard the Fun Car!

Best of Luck and Cheer
for Christmas and New Year
from ....

Bluejackets take a ride on a novel miniature car and trailer at a famous
East Coast holiday camp which has been taken over by the Admiralty,
camouflaged, and re-named H.M.S. Royal Arthur.

Hi-de-Hi! Chief Petty Officer!

find sites for other camps in North Wales and Scotland. After Dunkirk they wanted to be as far away as possible from the coast of northern France.

After motoring many hundreds of miles in his old Austin Ten car, Bill Butlin found two sites which he thought were ideal. One was in Pwllheli in Wales, the other in Ayr in Scotland. The Admiralty agreed, and very quickly the building began. After only three weeks, 8,000 naval ratings arrived at Pwllheli to find that the builders were still searching for water, and they had to sleep in tents.

The camp at Ayr was known as HMS Scotia, and the one at Pwllheli was HMS Glendower. Bill Butlin designed them, with an eye to turning them into holiday camps after the war. He put the parade ground, which could easily be dug up, where he wanted the swimming pool, he was so confident that the British would win.

Tyrolean Bar makes Sick Bay

The transformation from holiday camp to navy training camp was relatively easy. The buildings were already there, it was just a matter of adapting them for a very different use.

At Skegness, the Tyrolean bar was converted into a sick bay, and the dentist held his daily clinic under a sign which read, 'Mme Azalea, Fortune Teller'. The coloured fountains into which so many campers had fallen whilst singing 'Penny On The Drum', were shut down. All of the windows on the buildings were blacked out. The swimming pool, where happy campers had tumbled from the high diving board, was now used for navy boating drill and had a twelve oar cutter and six whalers, for rowing instruction.

After a farewell dinner of kidney soup, roast pork and golden sponge pudding, the Bluejackets set sail for the chill perils of the Atlantic convoys.

H.M.S. ROYAL ARTHUR

YE

OLD BUNTING TOSSERS

"CLASS S4"

FAREWELL DINNER

HILDREDS HOTEL, SKEGNESS

WEDNESDAY, NOVEMBER 27th, 1940

The comfortable beds, which had been used by the campers, with their pink and blue coverlets, were taken away. Space was all important, and to make room for four men to be able to sleep in a ten foot square chalet, metal framed, double-deck bunk beds were installed.

The chalets had originally been built only for use in summer but they were now going to be occupied all year round, including long cold winters. The chicken wire and distemper walls couldn't keep the cold out, and there was no heating in any of the other buildings on the camp. Naval ratings suffered badly from having to sleep in the bitterly cold chalets, and eat in the freezing dining halls.

It was so cold, that despite sleeping in their heavy overcoats, which they never seemed to take off, and sometimes two to a bed for warmth, they still woke up in the morning with a thin line of ice on their blankets where their breath had frozen. A lot of the men started going down with colds and 'flu, and the sick bays were overcrowded. To try and remedy the situation, braziers were put in the chalets but the fumes were too dangerous in such a confined space. Eventually the Admiralty installed tubular electric heaters in the chalets, and steam operated blow heaters in the dining halls.

The Butlin's Ingoldmells Hotel, which was built in 1938 next to the camp, and open to the public, became the officers' mess.

The Empress Ballroom, where Mantovani had played, was now used for issuing the shirts and uniforms, and the Palm Court lounge, where campers had sat quietly in comfortable wicker arm chairs, surrounded by gilt-edged mirrors, was turned into a classroom where naval ratings were given a crash course in seamanship.

The Windsor dining hall, which had echoed to the sound of a thousand campers shouting 'Hi-De-Hi' before breakfast, was now the chief petty officers' mess, and the other dining halls, York, Gloucester and Kent, were renamed the Forecastle, Top Deck and Quarterdeck.

King of Norway, right, leading to take the salute on the old skating rink

'Cough and drop 'em' in the Pirates' Cave.

Above the rooms being used by the training officers was the sign which was already famous to hundreds of Butlin's campers, 'Our True Intent Is All For Your Delight' and below it, new naval ratings pounded the parade ground.

The Navy dismantled the wooden stands round the stadium, where campers had cheered on the cheetah and greyhound races, because they needed the materials.

The main reception, where thousands of campers had come and gone, now had a gun above it. There were two more on the beach fronting the chalets, and two in the surrounding fields.

In the course of the war a quarter of a million men, including the Free French, the Norwegians and the Dutch, passed through the camp at Skegness. The King of Norway paid a visit and took the salute on the parade ground which was the site of the old skating rink.

During the war several bombs fell on the Skegness camp, and people were killed. In 1941 Lord Haw-Haw, who broadcast German propaganda, announced that HMS Royal Arthur had been sunk. In fact the Skegness holiday camp was unsinkable.

George Melly

In 1944 George Melly was one of the thousands of naval ratings sent to HMS Royal Arthur at Skegness. He thought he was going to an ordinary barracks, and hadn't any idea that it had previously been a Butlin's holiday camp.

When he arrived he was shown to his chalet, which like all the other buildings had been painted lead grey. But he noticed that some of the paint had peeled off, revealing little flashes of bright pink and lime green underneath. On the verandahs of each chalet, sailors were learning how to sling their hammocks, while the Tannoy system that had been previously used to wake campers up and tell them where the knobbly knees and Holiday Princess competitions were, now barked out orders.

George went to have a meal. All the buildings looked identical from the outside but the interiors hadn't been touched, as he soon discovered when he went to collect his 'irons' and found himself in what looked like a fake village pub, complete with the sign 'Ye Olde Pig & Whistle'. There was a Wren handing out cutlery through a mullioned window. He collected his food and went into the dining hall where he saw hundreds of naval ratings eating under a huge, fake plaster of paris tree, which looked as if it was growing from out of the floor, with its branches disappearing into the sky-painted ceiling. For a moment, George wondered if the surrealist movement that he was so keen on at the time, had taken over the Navy!

He was then sent for the regulation medical examination, which consisted of 'dropping your trousers and coughing.' This procedure took place in what had previously been the Pirates' Cave. George and a number of other sailors filed in to see the doctor, past the papier-maché skeletons embedded in fake rocks.

The camp cinema which every Friday night had shown films of campers winning competitions, entering races, being thrown in the pool, and just having a good time, now showed naval ratings films on the effects of venereal disease. It was a large cinema with a large screen and so were the images on it. George Melly recalls several men fainting, horrified at the sheer size of what they saw. There was also a film about cleaning your teeth, where owing to the size of the screen, the huge mouth and grubby finger massaging the gums, looked as if they belonged to a giant.

Many years later, when George Melly was in the Mick Mulligan Jazz Band, he played Sunday concerts back at Butlin's Skegness holiday camp. Although everything had been painted back to its jolly seaside colours, he was surprised how easily he could remember his way around.

Entertainer George Melly served in 1944 at HMS Royal Arthur, as Butlin's Skegness was called during the war years

The Tyrolean Bar became the sick bay

The Dungeon Bar became the canteen

In **Ye Olde Pig and Whistle Bar,** sailors collected their 'irons', knives and forks

Bill Bultin – adviser to Monty

Short Back And Sides

Molly Rowntree, who was the manageress of the hairdressing salon stayed to run it as a barber's shop. From 9.00 in the morning until 5.30 in the evening, the naval ratings queued to have their hair cut. Only a few weeks previously, she had been perming and waving women's hair ready for the camp dances in the evening. Now she was giving thousands of men identical regulation hair cuts, at a cost of four old pence. The Admiralty kept two pence.

The carefree holiday atmosphere of the camp that Molly had been used to, quickly disappeared, and she found it difficult to adjust to the rules and regulations now imposed on everyone. She spent a lot of time running into the air raid shelters, which were built where the rose beds had

In 1941 her salon was hit by a bomb and temporarily closed. Molly then moved to the new camp at Pwllheli, which hadn't ever been used as a holiday camp. When she arrived she found that there wasn't a salon so she had to use a makeshift marquee as a barbers. Unfortunately the biggest drawback was that it kept on blowing down, and after a few months Molly left to work in a fashionable hairdresser in London. She returned to Butlin's when the war ended.

Choking Unarmed Combat Instructor

One soldier who was stationed at Filey for the normal three weeks basic training, which consisted of square bashing, arms firing and grenade throwing, remembers one morning the instructor who was teaching unarmed combat choosing a big bloke for a demonstration. The instructor told him to grip his neck as hard as he could and for as long as he could. The man did, until the instructor started to turn blue and had to stop him. After the instructor had stopped spluttering and recovered, he asked the man what he did in civilian life. He confessed he was an all-in wrestler!

Prisoners of war settling down to a new life in prison 'somewhere in England'. Each one of these young men wears flannel trousers, pullover and jacket, and each a large coloured patch on knee and back of coat to identify him as a prisoner.

Butlin Makes 50,000 Women Happy

Whilst the camps at Pwllheli and Ayr were being built to Bill Butlin's specifications, Lord Beaverbrook gave him the unpaid job of Director General of Hostels.

This involved looking after some 50,000 women who were doing very necessary work in munitions factories all over the country. For security reasons these factories were situated away from towns and the women had to live in bleak hostel

In these gaily-painted huts – reminder of a carefree summer that now seems eons a

Bomb remains dropped on the sewage works, Skegness camp, 1940.

Germans who were interned for the duration of the war.

accommodation near by. Because they were miles away from any entertainment or social life and the evenings were lonely and boring, a lot of the women were leaving their jobs. Bill Butlin was told to find a way of giving them some entertainment, and making their living accommodation more comfortable.

He went and had a look at the Ordnance Hostels where these women were living and decided they should be run along similar lines to a basic holiday camp. He would provide good meals, a bar where they could have a drink, comfortable living accommodation and, most important of all, social events such as dances, whist drives, and amateur shows. He even made available a small plot of land for the women who liked gardening. His idea was very successful, and soon figures began to show that fewer women were leaving.

Bill Butlin, 'Tickled Pink'

In 1943 Basil Brown was Lieutenant Colonel, Assistant Director of Army Services. He realised early on in the war that a lot of the troops were talented music hall artists and comedians. He decided that they would be of more use entertaining the troops than being bad soldiers.

During the 'phoney war' of 1939 to 1940, he had put on concert parties to keep the bored troops amused. This gave him the idea of doing it on a national scale, and he formed a company called 'Stars In Battle Dress'.

One day Basil Brown's boss asked him if he knew Bill Butlin. Of course he had heard of him. Bill Butlin's expertise at organising mass entertainment of the type that people wanted had become well known, but he hadn't ever met him.

Colonel Basil Brown was told to go to London, see Bill Butlin and in the name of General Montgomery, invite him to be honorary advisor to the 21st Army Group covering all aspects of leave.

Bill Butlin was offered the job of finding suitable places on the coast around Europe for holiday camps and leave centres. The

Butlin Victorious – happy and glorious

idea was that Colonel Basil Brown would be Bill Butlin's 'minder' and whenever a major town was captured, the two of them would immediately go to the vicinity and take over suitable buildings and organise facilities for the troops coming back from the front line on either 48 hours or seven days leave. Bill Butlin was 'tickled pink', at the offer and immediately accepted.

The 21 Clubs

After the invasion of France, Bill Butlin was one of the first civilians to land there.

His job was to organise entertainment facilities. It quickly became apparent that the battle had moved inland, and troops who were pulled out of the line for 48 hours didn't have the time, or the ability, to travel to a holiday camp on the coast. Bill Butlin came up with the idea of requisitioning buildings inland and calling them '21 Clubs'. He took the name from the 21st Army Group and the famous club in New York.

These clubs were opened in France, Holland, Belgium and Germany. The last

---

The Wooden-Legged Barber of Butlin's

Within two years all five holiday camps were full. But just after the war Bill Butlin had a problem finding staff.

Molly Rowntree had returned to open a hairdressing salon on each camp and was having the same problem. She ended up having to employ one barber who was deaf and dumb, but turned out to be a wizard with a razor, and another one who had a wooden leg.

Bill Butlin got round the staff shortage by advertising a holiday-while-you-work scheme. This meant that people could come and stay on the camp for only two pounds two shillings a week, and in return they were expected to do four hours work a day.

Kathleen Parkinson was fourteen at the time, and was lucky enough to be one of the 24 boys and girls from her school who went for a six-week holiday at Butlin's camp at Filey. Like most of the children, she came from a working-class family and hadn't ever had a holiday. Such a long stay at Butlin's was a financial impossibility, but the headmaster of the school was a friend of Bill Butlin.

He came to an arrangement with him that the childrens' holiday was at a greatly reduced price and in return the children would pay for their keep by doing four hours work a day.

From Monday to Friday, they did the dusting, waited at the tables and the boys helped to carry the campers suitcases. Once their work was finished they were allowed to join in all the activities with the other campers.

Even finding pocket money for the children's holiday proved to be a problem. So before the holiday started the headmaster arranged for them to go in groups, three times a week, after school, to the head office of Butlin's in Oxford Street. For one shilling and sixpence an hour, they spent a couple of hours folding and packing brochures to be sent out to new campers.

The pay-as-you-work scheme wasn't really successful, because Bill Butlin's camps were so large that they needed an army of trained staff to make them run smoothly. He was relieved when millions of working men and women were demobilized and Butlin's were able to employ enough staff to run their camps efficiently.

one was in Hamburg.

Entry into the 21 Clubs was free, and food and drink was served at special reduced prices. Soldiers could go there and have a drink or see a show, and there were voluntary 'hostesses' who were described as 'ladies' who would dance with them to the music of local bands. The places were comfortable, and as well as dancing there was entertainment, billiards, table tennis and news from home.

The brother of the King of Belgium was on the committee, and members of the Belgian Royal Family came to help.

Everything that was available at a Butlin's holiday camp was to be found at the 21 Clubs, except for the seaside.

These Clubs were such a success, that in 1946 the Army High Command asked Bill Butlin to go and organise one for the troops in India. Unfortunately he was too busy back home, getting his holiday camps ready to reopen, so he sent Norman Bradford in his place. But the idea didn't come to anything.

Colonel Basil Brown and Bill Butlin worked together all through the war, and became great friends. When the war ended Bill Butlin offered him the job of Director of Entertainment for his holiday camps. Although Colonel Basil Brown hadn't ever seen a Butlin's holiday camp, let alone stayed at one, he accepted the job. Bill Butlin secured his release from the army just before the war ended, and Basil travelled by train to the camp at Filey. On the way he slipped into the lavatory and changed out of his uniform into civilian clothes, but he kept on his medals, and Bill Butlin insisted he should always be referred to as Colonel as he thought it was impressive on the Butlin's letter heading.

The day before war officially ended Bill Butlin arrived at his camp in Filey and celebrated VE (Victory in Europe) day with the troops. He had something else to celebrate. He'd got back his camps, not only the two at Skegness and Clacton but three new ones at Filey, Ayr and Pwllheli.

OPENING
The New Filey Camp
On the Yorkshire Coast

THE DATE YOU'VE WAITED FOR

2ND JUNE
1945

This folder, produced before the war, provided a glimpse of a great pre-war achievement 'Holidays with Play' in the Butlin way.

Filey was due to open in 1940. Old brochures were over-printed for the new opening in June 1945.

Bill Butlin bought up war surplus stocks of silk parachutes. Cut into triangles and overprinted with the Butlin motif, they sold as women's sun-tops.

Architect's Impression of

Fil

Opening

Occupying an

's Luxury Holiday Camp

Bay

sun 1940

over 190 Acres

'HI-DE-HI, HO-DE-HO, DOUSE THE LIGHTS AND AWAY WE GO!'

SUMMER LASTS LONGER AT

Butlin's LUXURY HOLIDAY CAMP

FILEY
(near Scarborough)

All Summer attractions in full swing right up to end of October.
INCLUSIVE TERMS:
Sept. £5:10:0 per week.
October £5:0:0 per week.

For vacant dates and booking forms apply

CELEBRITY WEEK
22-29 SEPT.
TOMMY HANDLEY AND
ITMA COMPANY

L.A.J. BUTLINS LTD.,
439 Oxford St., London, W.1

At the end of the war, there were still two hundred RAF men at Filey camp, but that didn't prevent Bill Butlin from organising his men to dismantle the air raid shelters and clear away the Nissen huts, whilst the Royal Engineers dragged up barbed wire from off the beaches and blasted away the concrete defence traps.

The country was in a joyous optimistic mood, people were glad to be alive and Bill Butlin sensed that they wanted to celebrate peace by going on holiday with their families. He wanted his camps to be ready to provide one for them, but first he had to get them in working order.

Two feet of mud had to be scraped from the bottom of the swimming pool and then it had to be cleaned and repainted. The parade ground was dug up and a boating lake was built in its place. The hundreds of chalets, which had been painted grey, were given a lick of bright Butlin's colours. In order to do it quickly even trainee managers were roped in to help.

The heaters that the Navy had installed to beat the winter cold were removed, because the camp now reverted back to summer use only. The campers came in at the same time as the new chalet furniture, chests of drawers, rugs and curtains. It was decided to leave the metal framed bunk beds, that had been put in for the troops, and each one was fitted with a brand new Dunlopillo mattress.

Ex-service men who came for a holiday at Butlin's just after the war, expecting the luxury of a double bed, groaned at the familiar sight of the bunk beds they'd spent the war years sleeping in.

Bye-bye Blues at Butlin's

When service personnel were demobbed they received a gratuity of several hundred pounds. Everyone was employed, even women. After six years of blackouts there was euphoria, they wanted fun and a holiday. Currency regulations made trips abroad impossible, petrol was rationed, so people headed for the train, the coast and Butlin's.

Within six weeks after the end of the war, the Butlin's camp at Filey was open for a short season. Thousands of holiday makers paid between £5 and £6 for a week's holiday. They arrived war-weary and tired. For a few weeks the holiday makers and the military personnel had to share the camp. When the RAF finally moved out, Bill Butlin took the salute and 10,000 campers and staff all wearing something red, white and blue marched across the parade ground behind the camp orchestra singing and waving flags.

They didn't seem to mind that the accommodation wasn't ready. One camper, given chalet R4, returned to reception to report, 'Delightful but it doesn't have a door.' Three hours later it did.

People came from all over the country, clutching their ration books which they left in reception. They queued for cigarettes, and were excited by the sight of fruit cake and ice cream, and a promise of chicken twice a week. They didn't have much money to spend, or special holiday clothes to wear or ideas of travelling abroad, a lot of them had been abroad and they were grateful to be home.

Some of them wore their old Skegness and Clacton camp badges. Some of them had the free holiday vouchers that they had been given when their holidays had been cut short because of the war in 1939.

Quiet Lounge at Butlin's

In the 1950s all the camps had quiet lounges, which held 200 people. In the one at Pwllheli the walls were covered with oil paintings, just some of the 400 that Bill Butlin bought during the war. He gave Christie's the auctioneers instructions that the paintings had to be large, and must not cost more than 50 guineas each. In 1982 the collection was said to be worth £5 million.

Culture at Filey

A year after the war ended Bill Butlin decided that he wanted his camps to have a new prestigious image. He chose to highlight the 250 acre camp site at Filey and as part of his big 'After The War' publicity promotion, he invited 400 guests, who included famous names in politics, art, music and London's social set. He paid £1,100 for the Yorkshire Pullman train to be taken out of storage, where it had been since the beginning of the war, and they were invited to make the train journey from Kings Cross Station to Filey camp.

When the guests arrived, Colonel Basil Brown had arranged for the San Carlos Opera Company to perform Puccini's *La Bohème* in the camp theatre.

Whilst the opera company were performing at Skegness, they stayed at the Butlin's Ingoldmells Hotel, next to the camp. The leading tenor was married to the leading soprano and one night in their room, they had a terrible argument. The walls were fairly thin and everyone could hear the shouting going on between them. Suddenly one of them sent for the manager and demanded that the double bed was removed from their room as they didn't want to sleep together. Of course, the manager had the double bed removed immediately, and twin beds were brought in. The next day, they called the manager and asked for the twin beds to be removed and the double bed to be returned.

The show was a great success, it didn't really matter whether the campers liked or disliked it, they filled the theatre with their curiosity and the event gave Butlin's a lot of publicity. The show ran at Skegness for a few weeks before moving onto the other camps.

Charlie the Elephant – so Big and Strong

'CHARLIE'S here at Butlin's Camp, a friend for one and all, he would simply love to have you come and pay a call.'

In 1957 Bill Butlin was on a plane returning home from the Bahamas, where he had opened a new hotel, when the stewardess handed him a daily newspaper. A story in the gossip column caught his eye. It was about Craigend Zoo being unable to afford the upkeep of Charlie, the biggest bull elephant in captivity, who was very expensive to feed. Although Tarzan had promised a donation of £250, the zoo were going to have to have Charlie destroyed unless they could find him a new owner.

Bill Butlin made a note of the story and when he arrived in London, the first thing he did was call his office and asked them to find out more details about Charlie the Elephant. He was told that the owners of the zoo were Andy and Willie Wilson, who Bill Butlin had known for years when they owned a pet shop in Glasgow. He called them and said that Charlie was now on the Butlin's payroll, as long as they could agree a purchase price and move him safely to the Butlin's camp forty miles away at Ayr.

No insurance company would cover the risk of transporting 5½ ton Charlie, who travelled to Ayr in an open low loader, with his trunk taking up the space of three lanes of traffic, and grabbing at passing lamp posts and traffic lights.

Four months after Bill Butlin made his offer, Charlie the Elephant and his keeper Shaik Ibrahim were safely installed at the camp at Ayr.

Charlie was a big hit, especially with the children. He and Ibrahim would walk round the camp and Ibrahim would take him down to the sea for a paddle.

A few months later it was decided that the camp at Ayr was too small for Charlie. Bill Butlin decided to move him to the camp 300 miles away at Filey. In May 1957 in the personal column of *The Times* newspaper there was an advertisement which read; 'Butlin's Ltd., will pay the sum of £1,000, cash, to any person able to arrange immediate safe transport of the largest elephant in captivity from Butlin's, Ayr (Scotland), to Butlin's, Filey (Yorkshire). Apply Butlin's Ltd., Luxury Holiday Camps, 439 Oxford Street, W.1.'

For the next few weeks this advertisement also appeared in the *Daily Telegraph*, the *Manchester Guardian* and the *Scotsman*. Butlin's received 3,500 replies. Some of the ideas were pretty bizarre and were filed under the heading 'screwball'. These included students from Nottingham Art College who suggested tying Charlie to a raft and floating him down to Filey. Other suggestions included getting Charlie to follow a female elephant who was on heat, putting him under hypnosis, employing the help of Superman, and taking him on a canal barge having first destroyed all the bridges.

A publisher suggested transporting him in a net attached to two helicopters. The Oxford University Department of Engineering Science proposed that a barrage balloon with girth belts should tow Charlie at an altitude of thirty feet above the road. A counter-proposal was that the camp at Filey should be moved to the elephant.

There were enough serious suggestion to fill three files headed Land, Air and Water. Bill Butlin realised that moving Charlie 40 miles to Ayr, which hadn't been easy, was nothing compared to the problems of moving him 300 miles.

Working on the theory that as he had

Above, Charlie's five-ton food truck for the 300-mile journey between Ayr and Filey. Right, Charlie arrives at Filey, exhausted after standing for 84 hours.

moved Charlie before he could move him again, Bill Butlin sent for Willie Wilson. Willie came up with an idea that none of the 3000 applicants had. Transport Charlie in a box. Charlie was 10ft high, 5ft wide and 12ft long and then there was his tremendous weight. It was going to require a very heavy box, pulled by a very powerful vehicle.

At a cost of £1,250, a box was made from 9 inch thick railway sleepers, sawn into eighteen foot lengths, bolted side by side. It was put on a Pickfords low loader. Charlie's feet were chained and he was smeared with lard to prevent him from rubbing himself sore on the inside of the box. Watched by the RSPCA and encouraged by his keeper Ibrahim, it took a whole day and a crate of apples to persuade Charlie to get into his box.

Ken Farmer was a Butlin's driver at Filey camp. His job was to drive a five-ton Bedford truck, with Charlie's food loaded on it, up to Ayr and travel back with the convoy. As Ayr camp came into sight, Ken had his first glimpse of Big Charlie enjoying a paddle in the sea with Ibrahim. Ken went to meet them and Charlie gave him a ride back to the camp site on his back.

'Big Charlie the Elephant, Bound for Butlin's Holiday Camp, Filey'

Once Charlie was safely in the box, accompanied by his faithful keeper Ibrahim, the convoy set off on its long journey to Filey. The route was lined by police with walkie-talkie radios. Because the convoy could only travel at ten miles an hour the journey took 3 days. It made newspaper headlines. As the convoy past through various towns, people came to see if they could catch a glimpse of Big Charlie.

The first night was spent near Edinburgh and Ibrahim shared an hotel room with Ken Farmer but for the other two nights he slept in the truck with Big Charlie.

Towards the end of the second day one car went ahead to find an hotel for the night. They stopped at a pub which had rooms and ordered drinks. They told the landlord they would like to stay and there were seven others arriving later. They ordered several large whiskies, rounds of sandwiches and fourteen buckets of water. When the landlord asked what the buckets of water were for, they replied, 'The elephant doesn't drink Scotch'.

Charlie had to arrive on the camp at Filey in daylight so that there could be maximum publicity. The convoy arrived at dawn and Charlie was taken to a field away from the camp site where he was eventually coaxed out of his box. He looked pretty dreadful which wasn't surprising. After all he had been standing for 84 hours, virtually in the dark. He blinked slowly and moved backwards carefully. Someone got on a ladder and swept his back with a broom and by the time the campers had finished their breakfast Charlie was on the site. He was met by the camp mayor wearing his full regalia, brass chain and cotton wool ermine robes and hundreds of children who had been issued with union jacks.

Charlie lived in a specially built elephant house and was very good with children. One day Ted Young, who ran Filey camp, received a phone call from Bill Butlin, telling him that he wanted Ibrahim to teach Charlie to paint. 'The chalets?' asked Ted. 'No, not the chalets.' Bill Butlin had read a newspaper report about a monkey in America who painted pictures with its feet. He wanted Charlie to paint a painting by holding a brush in his trunk. Ted thought they had all gone mad. But he followed Bill Butlin's strict instructions and told Ibrahim to teach Charlie to paint. Charlie started off with a broom and a bucket of distemper and the wall of his wooden elephant house. One stroke of the

Big Charlie with his keeper Shaik Ibrahim at Ayr 1957.

Above, Sybil (centre) who 28 years later was midwife to Ringo Starr's first grandchild.

broom, and the elephant house was gone!

Eventually after a couple of months Ibrahim had taught Charlie to hold a two-foot long paint brush and Bill Butlin came to see the progress. He wasn't very impressed by the two-foot long paint brush and produced from his pocket a small artist's brush which he instructed Ibrahim to give to Charlie to hold. Ibrahim protested that Charlie wouldn't do it, but Bill Butlin insisted. Ibrahim gave Charlie the small paint brush, and he instantly ate it.

Ibrahim and Charlie were inseparable. They lived together and shared everything, from a bottle of whisky to a cake which Ted Young's wife used to make. When

Ibrahim was taken ill and died, Charlie pined so badly that shortly afterwards the RSPCA had to destroy him.

Another Butlin's elephant was Gertrude who was bought from London Zoo in the 1960s. Gertrude went to the camp at Pwllheli, but she was particularly difficult. After only a few months she was moved at night by Pickfords to Skegness, because there was an elephant trainer called Steve there, who they thought could control her.

When Gertrude arrived at Skegness there was no publicity and she was hustled into an elephant shed for two weeks before being brought out to meet the campers. Unfortunately Gertrude didn't behave well. She charged wildly through the camp, trumpeting loudly with Steve running after her. For the next few weeks every time Gertrude was taken out she behaved badly, and was so nervous that she made the most terrible messes all over the camp site.

Terry Rainsford was working on the licensed bars. That summer he was moved to the Butlin's hotel as a trainee manager and he had the responsibility of getting up at 6 o'clock every morning to let the cleaners in. He would see Steve take Gertrude the elephant to the shallow end of the swimming pool, where she would kneel down and he would wash her head. One morning Terry was watching Gertrude being washed when he realised that Steve was getting very agitated. Gertrude eased her way past him and slowly walked into the deep end of the pool with her trunk waving in the air. Steve was getting frantic and started throwing wooden deck chairs that were round the edge of the pool at the elephant but she just carried on walking, until she suddenly dropped her trunk and keeled over. Steve began to cry and Terry ran across to the pool to find him sobbing 'Gertrude's dead.' It was discovered later that she had suffered a heart attack.

The water started to turn a murky brown colour and half an hour later the camp was in pandemonium, which wasn't surprising. It isn't often campers wake up and find a elephant dead in the swimming pool. Tarpaulins were arranged around the pool and security men positioned on top of the buildings because Butlin's didn't want any press coverage.

A crane was sent for and when it eventually arrived it was put near the diving board. But someone was needed to dive into the brown murky water of the pool and shackle the elephant's legs in order to be able to lift it out. A Redcoat lifeguard volunteered, and was paid an extra £5.

The first effort to get the elephant out failed because the crane crashed and it had to be jacked up before it finally managed to heave Gertrude the elephant out of the pool.

Steve sobbed throughout the whole proceedings and when Gertrude was taken away in the back of a lorry, he claimed her foot as a hat stand.

Charlie the Elephant

CHORUS

You've heard of ugly ducklings,
and Reindeers in the snow,
here's the story of an Elephant
you would like to know.

He's Charlie the Elephant,
he's so big and strong,
Charlie the Elephant,
he can do no wrong,
He's a great big fellow,
he'd make a lovely toy,
there should be a Charlie
for every girl and boy.
Charlie's here at Butlin's camp,
a friend for one and all,
he would simply love to have you
come and pay a call
and when you smile or wave hello
to this big gentle pet,
keep saying 'Good Old Charlie'
'cause elephants never forget!

SKEGNESS

SKEGNESS

Haw Haw said the Germans had sunk it. It can accommodate 8,800.

CAMP

Night Owls

During the day children were catered for at Butlin's with a 'kiddies' paddling pool, seesaws, swings and a sand pit. Bill Butlin realised that there was no point in providing evening entertainment for parents if they could't safely leave their children. He was trying to attract families to his camp and decided to offer them a free baby-minding service. In the evenings Butlin's nurses on bicycles would constantly patrol the chalet lines. If they heard a baby crying they would make note of the chalet number, and report it back to the main office. Immediately someone was sent with this information to all the bars, theatres and dance halls on the camp site, where there were huge boards which read, 'Baby Crying in Chalet Number –' and the appropriate chalet number with the crying baby in it would be displayed. Over the years the 'Baby crying' board has changed to a flashing sign, but fifty years later the same child-minding system still remains.

Life with Uncle Boko

The most famous Butlin's 'Uncle' was Uncle Boko who started at Skegness after the war and died in his chalet in the late 1960s. He always wore a red fez hat, and did a magic act. Even today there is an 'Uncle' on all the Butlin's sites. His job is to be master of ceremonies for children's competitions.

P 133

Shirley Butlin

invites

Norman Chris Simpson

to

a Birthday Party

at

Her Daddy's Holiday Camp,

on

Friday, September 25th, 1936.

TEA at 5
✠
ENTERTAINMENT
till 9.

You Are Invited To My Daddy's Camp

Since Bill Butlin had first arrived in Skegness ten years earlier, he had grown very fond of the place, and the people. As if to prove it, he invited all the local schoolchildren to his daughter Shirley's fifth birthday party on the camp. Hundreds of them turned up, and they were all given a free tea on the lawn, and a present to take home.

BADGES

Retain Your Badges, They Will Become Your Passport To Winter Happiness

Because of the licensing laws all the campers had to wear a little metal badge to prove they were members of the Butlin's club and could be served with food and drink, and wander freely in and out of the camp. Camp badges weren't a new idea. Cunningham's Young Men's Holiday Camp had issued them to campers for a penny in the early 1920s. In 1936, when the first Butlin's badge was produced campers had to pay a shilling for it when they booked in at reception. Shortly afterwards the badges were free.

These badges became so popular with the campers that a new design was bought out every season and later on, a different one for every camp. After a while it was discovered that people who hadn't paid to stay at Butlin's were getting hold of the badges from ex-campers, and wandering freely in and out of the site, and using the facilities. In order to stop this the designs of the badges were altered slightly two or three times during the season.

The only time the production of badges was stopped was during the war, but they continued immediately afterwards, and in 1945 a badge was issued at Filey camp with a 'V for Victory' sign on it. The majority of them were made by two badge companies in Birmingham, Fattorini & Sons and J. R. Gaunt & Son. They also produced the designs, which were based on either a holiday or pictorial theme of the area where a particular camp was situated. The designs would be shown to Bill Butlin, who made the final choice.

Campers collected badges and wore them from previous years pinned in rows down their jacket lapels, or if they had too many, pinned to a scarf and hung round their necks. They wore them as souvenirs when they returned home after their holiday, and they served as a free advertisement for the camp.

As well as the general camp badges special ones were introduced for various clubs and events. The first of these just after the war, were the Beaver Club and the Albert Hall reunion badges, followed by Dance festivals, the 913 Club, and the 15 Club both of which were for children – there were badges for campers committee members, day members, Christmas, the Car and Cycling Clubs, the Choral Society, Social Club and for campers who stayed for more than one week. Members of the Butlin's staff, whose jobs ranged from nursing to gardening, all wore different badges.

Apart from the Beaver and 913 Clubs, Butlin's stopped issuing badges in 1967 because of the cost and because they said women preferred not to have pin marks in their clothes. There are no records as to the number of badges Butlin's produced over the years, although considering the number of camps and the number of campers, it must have run into thousands, with thousands of types and different colour combination for clubs, camps and hotels.

Right, Skegness car badge

SKEGNESS When the camp opened in 1936, it had a stadium which could seat 4,000. It was used every Friday for pig and cheetah and greyhound racing. The cheetahs, who always won, were kept in an area at the far end of the site, where campers could also leave their pets.

the Best holiday we've ever had

... I'm sure you'll like Butlin's

CLACTON At the opening ceremony Lord Castlerosse made a speech to the crowds. He told them 'Bill Butlin has done more for England than St George'. Clacton was the first camp to open for Christmas it was so cold all the pipes froze. Only the campers who complained were given an oil stove.

FILEY The San Carlo Opera Company performed Puccini's La Bohème at the opening. The Old Vic company put on a season of Shakespeare plays. Filey had its own station, Charlie the Biggest Bull Elephant in captivity and a bar that was an exact replica of one at the House of Commons.

ANTI-FRAUD. The passports to the camp and activities were badges. To prevent them being sold colour variations to the same design were introduced.

AYR Opened by Sir Harry Lauder. Ronnie Munroe directed the resident dance orchestra. All the Redcoats wore kilts. Bill Butlin's son, Bobby was a Redcoat at Ayr during his school holidays, when he was sixteen. In 1948 Butlin's opened the Heads of Ayr Hotel, next to the camp.

PWLLHELI Built during the war on the Welsh coast, out of the range of Hitler's bombs, it was used by the Navy. It opened every year for the annual Eisteddfod. The Butlin's Active Teens Scheme which provides 13 to 16-year-olds a chance to do abseiling, orienteering and fencing is held at Pwllheli.

MOSNEY After the war rationing was still in force but not in Southern Ireland. This meant that holidaymakers who stayed on the camp at Mosney used to send food parcels home to their families in England. In 1954 Hopalong Cassidy visited the camp and all the children dressed up as cowboys.

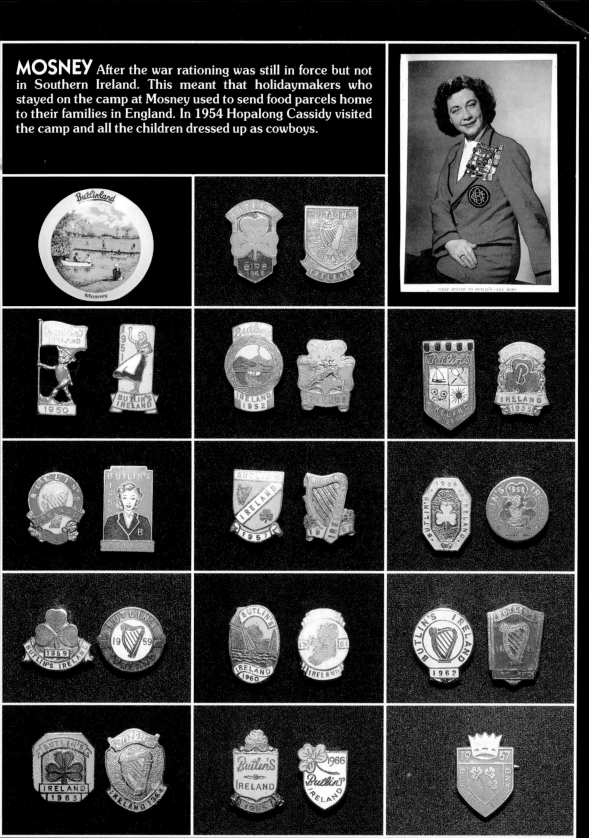

CHIEF HOSTESS TO BUTLIN'S—KAY BURY

BOGNOR Flooding caused by heavy rain meant the camp was not finished by the time it opened. Campers were offered alternative accommodation at Clacton. Those who stayed helped to fix the chalet doors and window frames. They received a free bottle of champagne. It was the first camp to be built with private bathrooms.

MINEHEAD 150,000 roses were planted. To prevent flooding from the surrounding marshland, a moat was built round the outside of the camp, 30ft wide, 10ft deep and a mile long. It became the boating lake. In 1986 it is to be relaunched as Somerwest World at a cost of £9 million.

BARRY A darts tournament is held every Easter. In the spring thousands of French and English schoolchildren use the camp for Venture Weeks. During one week in the summer, 35,000 pieces of bacon and 12,000 eggs are cooked for breakfast. There is a special room for preparing the 3 tons of potatoes eaten every week.

Joe

FOOD AT BUTLIN'S – 'LEGS ELEVEN. WHAT A SMASHER! TWO FRIED EGGS AND A GAMMON RASHER'

Before the war Butlin's served four meals a day. It advertised as a 'typical day's fare': **Breakfast:** Grapefruit, Bacon and Eggs, Bread and Butter, Marmalade and Tea. **Lunch:** Roast Leg of Lamb, Mint Sauce, Beans, Roast and Boiled Potatoes, Fruit Tart and Custard, Bread and Butter. **Tea:** Brown and White Bread and Butter, Jam and Cakes. **Dinner:** Soup, Steamed Salmon and Cucumber, Blancmange, followed by Cheese. The vegetables were served in silver tureens and the lady campers wore long frocks, ready to dance the Butlin's Ballet, when dinner was finished.

The chef, Joe Velich, was everyone's image of how a chef should look. A big, rounded jolly person, he used to walk around the dining hall wearing his big white chef's hat and overalls, chatting to the campers. There were some who said he never cooked anything but was just a front-of-house chef, but it didn't matter. He was as popular with the campers as the food he served. In between meal-times he refereed the boxing matches and posed for photographs with the Butlin's bathing beauties.

Although there was no room service at Butlin's and campers were woken with a 'wakey wakey' call to get them all into breakfast on time, they were able to have early morning tea in their chalets. When they arrived at reception they would buy a book of tea vouchers which entitled them to a cup of tea from the yellow and blue coloured tea trolley, which played musical bells in order to let campers know that it was outside their chalet line. It served tea like 'Mother used to make', and in between meals it went around ready to serve thirsty campers. 'No wonder that Butlin's, like tea, is a household word'.

> 'Early in the morning
> Before you start the day,
> Tea revives – and quickly drives
> The mists of sleep away.'

Later on in the 1950s campers could take a large thermos flask to the canteen in the morning and for one shilling and sixpence it would be filled with tea or coffee and they could take it and some paper cups back to their chalet.

How Do you want your Cornflakes? Fried or Boiled?

After the war campers brought their ration books to Butlin's, handed them in at reception and collected them when they left. The teatime of bread and jam and cakes was stopped and campers were served with breakfast plus two three-course meals a day. Snack bars, cafes, ice cream parlours and milk bars opened up which served cakes and cheese, spam and dried egg sandwiches, but the cost of these was not included in the price of the holiday. Campers would queue for the luxury of a slice of fruit cake or an ice cream and there was a whole generation of war-time children who had their first taste of bacon, as well as live bands, at Butlin's.

In 1947 Margaret Wilson went to Butlin's at Filey. She remembers the luxury of being given eggs and bacon every morning, at home they were only served on Sunday and bread and dripping during the week. She also thought it was great to have meat every day at Butlin's and a second helping if you were still hungry. It wasn't just a second helping, but a complete second meal.

Because of rationing mass catering was a problem. Fresh eggs were supplied from local farmers near each camp, but powdered egg was used for making cakes and sandwiches. Whale meat was put in steak and kidney pie or garnished with onions, and the campers were told it was 'Canadian wind-dried steak'. There were a lot of potatoes, spam and fish, which came from nearby Grimsby and Hull and was either fried, boiled and baked. A pot of tea was always served with the soup. Molly Rowntree suggested to Bill Butlin that they should serve the tea at the end of the meal, so he

73

In 1984 600 tons of chips, 97,000 doz. eggs, 86,000 doz. hamburgers

Stan Morse, top left and friends

Gallons of Soup of the day

agreed to give it a try. After only three days there was a deputation of campers demanding their tea back, and even today tea is served at the beginning of the meal.

'My Name is Stan. I am Your Waiter'

Stan Haines was a waiter at Butlin's for 36 years. He started in Skegness in 1946, the first season it opened after the war. The meals were served in two sittings, so as to accommodate all the thousands of campers. Each waiter looked after six tables with four campers on each. Stan would walk round the dining room in the mornings and introduce himself, 'My name is Stan. I am your waiter. I hope you have a nice holiday with Mr Butlin. If you have any complaints I am the man to rectify them.'

The tables were covered with plastic cloths and for speed all the food was served already on the plates. Waiters were taught to carry eight plates at a time and had round shoulders by the end of the season. The Jackson food trolley was introduced in 1939. It was the only way that 4,000 hot meals could be served quickly. The food was dished up on to the plates and kept in the thermostatically heated trolleys, each one held 120 plates. The racks were taken out and the meals were served immediately. In the early days the trolleys were wheeled into the dining room and plugged

> **Sunday 1985**
> Country Vegetable Soup
> a. Roast Topside of Beef, Yorkshire Pudding, Buttered Cabbage, Mixed Vegetables, Roast and
> Boiled Potatoes
> *or*
> b. Grilled Pork Chop and Apple Sauce Garden Peas, Grilled Tomato, French Fried Potatoes
> *or*
> c. Ham and Mushroom Pizza Garden Peas, Grilled tomato, French Fried Potatoes
> *or*
> d. Salmon with Summer Salad
> —oOo—
> (a) Dutch Apple Pie with custard Sauce
> *or*
> (b) Fruit Salad and Dairy Cream

into sockets suspended from the ceiling, but later they were kept in the kitchens.

At the Clacton camp before the war there were potato peelers, bread slicers, bacon and meat cutters, refrigerators and five large washing-up machines that could clean 8,000 pieces of china an hour. The kitchens were cleaned at night and huge ventilating fans kept the air free of cooking smells.

'How did You find Your Fish?' 'I Moved the Chip and it was There'

Just after the war, haddock tails were served for breakfast but after four weeks the campers were given bacon. Soup was served

74

were eaten, 700,000 pints of beer drunk at the six Butlin's centres

Above, Plating up meals at Butlin's. It takes five minutes for 22 waitresses to serve a thousand people with soup

Butlin's so fast food, it's gone!

with both main meals and there was salad and sometimes rabbit. Sunday lunch would be roast beef. Dinner, or evening meal as it was then called, was tinned salmon and salad followed by a piece of cake. To campers who had lived with months of rationing, the food at Butlin's was wonderful. No alcohol was served in the dining room, except at Christmas, when the chef would appear carrying a huge pudding and there would be fruit and nuts and wine.

Waiters wore a black bow tie and a short white 'monkey' jacket with blue cuffs and matching blue lapels. They had to supply their own black shoes and trousers. The paper shirt fronts and collars cost one penny each. In overtime a waiter could earn five shillings for working a couple of hours, plucking chickens or skinning rabbits, as well as getting one pound in tips every week, from every table that they looked after.

When the evening meal was finished the waiters had to put the tables outside and line up the chairs in front of the stage ready for the evening entertainment. Whilst they were washing up in the kitchen the campers would shout out for them to be quiet because they couldn't hear the comedians for the clatter of knives and forks. In 1954 they stopped holding shows in the dining rooms.

Holiday Camps Come-of-Age

To mark the 21st anniversary of Butlin's Ltd, this giant cake was displayed in Butlin's Ocean Hotel, Brighton. The foundation was made of hardboard, the icing was by the head patissier at the Ocean Hotel, Mr Townsend, who spent 8 hours in hand piping the design of roses and laurel leaves. 16lb of sugar and 40 whites of egg were used for the icing. The cake weighed about 30lb and was 14 in. in diameter. Coloured views of the hotel were set in the icing, with a bust of holiday camp 'King' Billy Butlin on the top tier.

75

Navy. It covers 250 acres in north Wales, and can accommodate 9,300 people.

Disasters

Barry 1968 The Beachcomber Bar, the biggest bar in Europe, caught fire.

Turkish baths gutted

Pre-war Butlin's had their own fire brigade with uniforms and a fire engine. It was needed. During the winter of 1938 a Skegness store room where the mattresses were kept caught fire. The Turkish baths were gutted and never rebuilt.

During the flood at Skegness in 1953 the mattresses got soaked and the army were sent in with huge blow dryers. After the mattresses had dried out there were water marks on them. New ones were ordered for Skegness, whilst the old ones with the water stains were sent up to the camp at Pwllheli. Bill Butlin decided that as there hadn't been a flood up there, no one would lift the sheets to check the mattresses.

In 1971 Minehead suffered a fire in the Blinking Owl Bar and Playhouse Theatre – the camp did not close.

Butlin's Do–It–Yourself

After the war Bill Butlin bought up large quantities of surplus stocks from the government and utilized them on his camps. He bought aeroplane seats from old bombers and put them round the swimming pools. The small model wooden aeroplanes which had been used to train the Observer Corps to identify different types of aircraft, were hung as decorations in all the camp bars. The bar stools were made from upside down bomb cases. The huge mirrors in the ballroom at Bognor were taken from inside search lights. The triangles of silk which were used by parachutists to guide them to their landing, were printed with the word Butlin's and sold as suntops. Bill Butlin bought up various job lots of strange items such as plastic salad shakers in to which he put a light bulb and hung around the camp sites as if they were fairy lights. The giant plaster guardsmen outside the Butlin's Ocean Hotel in Brighton, and the knights on horseback in the Butlin's theatres were old Regent Street Christmas decorations.

Pwllheli where a fire in 1973 destroyed the main building. Ken Dodd was appearing in the Midnight Cabaret.

Skegness June 1974, The Princess Building, incorporating the Beachcomber Bar, Princess Ballroom, amusement arcades and shops, caught fire. The camp did not close.

Skegness January 1953, 257 were drowned in a flood. Campers were found sitting on their top bunks to try to stay above the water.

d Tennis Courts from Sand Dunes
Skegness Holiday Camp

Jolly Boating Weather Building the Butlin's camp was almost complete when a local farmer showed Bill Butlin a photograph of the site, taken thirty years previously. Everywhere was flooded under five foot of water, which was caused by high tides crashing over the sand dunes. This apparently happened every fifteen years, and Bill Butlin was horrified when the locals around Skegness recalled the last time the area had flooded was fourteen years before. He decided he had better reinforce the sea wall in order to protect his camp. Building stopped whilst thousands of tons of soil were dug out, leaving a large hole on the camp site, 50 feet wide and 2,000 feet long. It was quickly decided to turn it into the boating lake.

79

AYR covers 85 acres and can accommodate 5,400. It has its own railway station.

Hello Ma'am!

Your Royal Highness, Lords, Ladies and Campers

Over the years apart from thousands of ordinary holiday makers Butlin's had visits from aristocrats, Members of Parliament and Royalty. The first royal visitor was the Duchess of Gloucester in 1939, who happened to be in Skegness to open a hospital. Bill Butlin, spotting the potential publicity from a royal visit, invited her to his holiday camp. She accepted his invitation and during a tour of the site she planted a tree, and opened the Gloucester House Dining room.

The second royal visitor was Prince Philip, who was stationed at the camp at Pwllheli when he was a young sailor during the war. Years later when Bill Butlin was at Buckingham Palace the Queen told him that her young children were always asking her when they could visit a holiday camp. They never did, but in 1963 the Queen visited the camp at Pwllheli where her husband had been stationed. Whilst they were touring the site Bill Butlin asked Prince Philip which chalet was his, but Prince Philip refused to tell him saying jokingly that if Bill Butlin knew he'd probably put up a sign and charge people to go and look at it!

In the late 1940s, Chalet A7 at Filey, which was exactly the same as all the others, was reserved for visiting VIPs. Lord Dalton, who was then Chancellor of the Exchequer, stayed there for a week to attend the Labour Party League of Youth conference. Lord Avon, then Sir Anthony Eden stayed whilst at he Young Conservatives conference at he camp. Mr Hugh Gaitskell, Sir William Lawther and his wife Lady Violet Bonham Carter, Countess Mountbatten and her daughter Pamela, and Princess Alexandra, all stayed on the camp site.

Lord Dalton

Sir Anthony Eden

Duchess of Glouce

Right, Countess Mountbatten, second from left.
Far right, The Queen and Prince Philip, Pwllheli 1963

82

Parliament Bar, Filey, a replica of the real one at Westminster   Hugh Gaitskell, Filey

Skegness 1939

IRELAND

It was the first to be called a 'Holiday Village'. It was sold in 1982.

THE CHURCH ON HOLIDAY

'Bill Butlin wanted his camps to be like self-contained villages and his campers to be able to do everything on holiday that they could do at home. This is why, as well as providing meals and entertainment, there were also shops, a laundry, a shoe-shine service, and a doctor's surgery. The only thing that was missing was a church and if the campers wanted to go to one they had to travel to the nearest town.

In 1937 Reverend Colin Davies, then vicar of Ingoldmells, was appointed Senior Chaplin to the Butlin organisation but he left after one season to work abroad. The job was taken on in 1947 by Reverend Tom Pugh. He retired in 1960 and his assistant, Reverend Clifford Malkenson, or Father Cliff as he preferred to be called, took over the job. When he started as assistant padre to the camps, Father Cliff used to help Reverend Pugh visit all the camps, which as well as Clacton, Filey and Skegness now included Ayr, Pwllheli and Mosney in Ireland.

Father Cliff would have his breakfast early so that he could wander round the dining room and talk to the campers whilst they ate theirs. He always wore his cassock so that he was easily identifiable.

On a Saturday morning when the new campers arrived, he would greet them in reception and then wander round the swimming pool signing authographs with the words, 'God Bless you'. At 6.30 that evening in the Gaiety Theatre the Entertainments Manager would tell the new campers the rules and introduce them to various members of the Butlin's staff. It was called 'Who's Who'.

When it was Father Cliff's turn the band would play, 'He's Got The Whole World In His Hands' and Father Cliff would come onto the stage and give the campers greetings from the church and tell them the times of the services and that if they had any problems they could talk to him in his chalet from eleven till one each lunch time.

It was mostly women who came to see him, up to 80 in a week, bringing with them their marital problems. He would often ask them to return with their husbands but they generally didn't. Sometimes he would write to their local parish priest asking them to follow up the case, but as his meetings were in confidence it wasn't possible to pass on the details.

There were two masses every day that fitted in round the mealtimes and on Sunday, at 10.30 in the morning, there was a non-denominational service in the Gaiety Theatre. At first this was called 'The People's Service' but when sponsorship started the campers thought the service was sponsored by *The People* newspaper, so it was changed to 'The Holiday Service'. There was no other activities going on at the time and the campers would turn out in their hundreds, all casually dressed in their holiday clothes.

At the harvest thanksgiving service there would be a full orchestra and as many as 2000 in the congregation. The sermons were short, as the campers liked to sing, and Redcoats took the collection.

During the week Father Cliff judged competitions, the Glamorous Grandmother, the Mother and Child (which was his favourite), the Holiday Princess and Fancy Dress. The most popular costume was Miss Poland, which was a child with a potty on its head, wearing a costume made of lavatory paper.

Along with the nurse and the head of the sick bay, he judged the Bonnie Baby competition. This would cause him some embarrassment when later on in the week he would bump into a baby on the camp and casually comment what a pretty child it was and the mother would reply, 'That's not what you thought on Monday when you judged the Baby Competition.'

Over the years conferences of clergymen were held on the camps. In 1953 the Archbishop of York visited the camp at Filey and had tea in the Palm Court Restaurant with Godfrey Winn, Bill Butlin

Above, Father Cliff gives 1st prize to the Yellow Rose of Texas. Right and below, one of the many religious conferences at Filey. On cycles: Lord Halifax and the

Bishop of Hull, behind, the Bishop of Ceylon, Lebrombo, Upper Nile, & Willochra, with the Centenary Queens of Liverpool.

and his wife and Countess Mountbatten who was spending a few days at the camp with her daughter Pamela.

Father Cliff drove many thousands of miles during the summer season, checking that the padres were coping with the campers, the services and competitions.

If there was a death on the camp Butlin's would organise the undertakers and make facilities available for the bereaved holiday maker to phone their relatives and return home.

Confirmation classes were held on the camps for Redcoats and the Bishop of Grantham would come and take the confirmation service. About 8 babies were christened every season, usually the parents had first met on holiday at Butlin's.

Over the years hundreds of romances stared on the camp, including one between a Miss Pot and a Mr Kettle who eventually married. About 5 couples a year would have their marriages blessed in the camp church. They were usually Redcoats and if they paid extra they could have a wedding reception in the Golden Grill.

BUTLIN'S BOGNOR REGIS
The Children's Playground and Fun Fair

BUTLIN'S BOGNOR REGIS
The Reception Hall

BOGNOR accommodates 4,300. It has more day visitors than any other site.

BUTLIN'S BOGNOR REGIS
A Carousel Pig and Whistle Bar

BUTLIN'S BOGNOR REGIS
Fountain and Heated Outdoor Pool

Every year Butlin's sponsor a Birdman contest to see who can fly farthest from the end of the pier.

Mushie the toothless wonder lion

'MUSHIE' The LION AT BUTLINS

Great Lion Hunt: Holiday Makers Armed With Rifles

In the 1930s Bill Butlin introduced lions to his amusement sites. He was very fond of them, and used to drive round Skegness in his Austin Seven car with a lion cub sitting in the back. His affection for lions club began with one called Rex. Rex travelled by lorry, with some other animals from Skegness, to the Butlin's zoo which was on the amusement site in Bognor. Rex was Butlin's only lion at the time, so they had to make him go round. When the lorry arrived all the animals were there except for Rex, who appeared to be missing. Before Bill Butlin had time to check whether or not Rex had actually been loaded onto the lorry in Skegness, a local newspaper reporter asked him if he'd lost a lion. Bill Butlin said that it looked as if he had, and the following day the local newspaper carried a story about a 'Butlin's Lion On The Loose'. There followed several days of intense press coverage, which included Bill Butlin and a fleet of press cars with reporters hanging out of every window, hunting all over West Sussex for a lion. The newspaper headlines became more serious; 'Great Lion Hunt. Holiday Makers Armed With Rifles' read one. The locals were scared, the schools were closed and the Territorial Army was called out to join in the search. Things were certainly getting serious when a newspaper reported that one man slept with a twelve bore shot gun by his bed. Then a local farmer rang Bill Butlin's office and nervously told him that one of his sheep had been badly mauled by a lion.

To his relief Bill Butlin discovered that it couldn't have been Rex, because Rex was still in Skegness, where he hadn't ever been loaded on to the lorry. But the whole episode had turned out to be such a good publicity stunt that Bill Butlin just couldn't stop it. So he allowed the stories to continue for a few more days, until he decided it was time he produced a happy

ending to it all. Rex was brought down to Bognor at the dead of night, and the plan was that Bill Butlin would announce that Rex the lion had been recaptured and was now safely behind bars. Everyone could relax and normal life could resume.

Unfortunately when Rex arrived in Bognor, he looked in the best of health, and nothing like a lion who was supposed to have been roughing it in Sussex ditches for the last few days. Bill Butlin thought that Rex had to be made to look bedraggled and miserable, and in order to achieve the required effect he threw a bucket of green distemper over him. Of course it worked. Covered in green distemper Rex looked as if he'd been rolling in the dirtiest ditches, and wandering in the filthiest fields. He was put on show, safely behind bars, looking suitably miserable. That should have been the end of the story, but unfortunately it wasn't.

The reporter who had written the original newspaper article, Bill Butlin, the manager of his Bognor zoo and the owner of the dead sheep were all charged with 'conspiracy to commit a public mischief by certain false statements that a lion had escaped'. The case lasted for two days, and for two nights all the accused were kept in the cells. The result was that the reporter was fined £30 for exaggerating the story and the farmer was fined £10 for planting the dead sheep. Bill Butlin and his zoo manager were found 'Not Guilty' and given costs. When it was all over the first thing Bill Butlin did was to send a telegram to his mother who was at Olympia, which read, 'Justice has been done'. She replied by telegram, 'Appeal at once'.

Mushie The Toothless Lion

Mushie was another lion on the Butlin amusement site. But he didn't cause anything like the stir or the notoriety that Rex had. Mushie was very old and very tame. During the day time he would sit, looking very docile, outside his trainer's caravan.

None of the fairground people were frightened of Mushie, they were more frightened of the trainer's little Jack Russell terrier who was known to bite. Fortunately Mushie wasn't able to bite anyone, because he didn't have any teeth, which was why his trainer was quite happy to stick her head in its mouth as part of their act.

The Butlin's zoo on the Skegness amusement site had six lions, three bears, one of which danced, a leopard, monkeys, a kangaroo and several seals. Amongst the side shows was Professor Rousseau's Performing Flea Circus, Madame Hart's Mental Telepathy Show and an African village with Naomi, the snake charmer.

After the war there was a weekly raffle on the camp for a car. The winner was offered cash for it. Because most people couldn't drive and petrol was rationed, they usually accepted the cash in place of the car. The same car was raffled every two weeks.

Beware! Smelly Dog. The camp sewage farm was another problem. Bill Butlin hadn't ever designed one before and even though it was some distance away at the back of the camp, the smell was, to say the least, a bit strong. Bill Butlin decided that the high wall around the sewage farm might not be enough to deter curious campers attracted by the stench, so he put up a large notice, which read 'Beware of the dog'. One day a new camper walked up to Bill Butlin and pointing in the direction of the sewage said, 'You know that dog down there – it doesn't half smell.'

MINEHEAD

Christmas. In 1986 it will have 487 new de-luxe apartments and a caravan park.

Butlin's Caribbean Calypso

In 1948 Bill Butlin paid nearly half a million pounds for the Fort Montague Hotel in Nassau and he spent £100,000 on modernising it. Two months later he bought the Princess Hotel in Bermuda for £325,000. In 1949 he started a public company called, Butlin's (Bahamas) Ltd., so that he could open a Vacation Village for American tourists on the Grand Bahamas. When it opened in 1950, the buildings were unfinished. Six months later the company collapsed and was wound up by the liquidator. Bill Butlin and his backers lost a great deal of money.

There were a number of reasons for the failure. Firstly, the project cost more to build than the local estimates had first indicated. Secondly, an attempt to cover the loss by introducing a gambling casino never got off the ground. Thirdly, the project was years ahead of its time. Middle class Americans hadn't yet got into the mass holiday market.

Even though the project collapsed, those shareholders in Butlins (Bahamas) Ltd. who also held shares in Butlin's British company covered their losses by the rise in each share from £1 in 1949 to £50 twelve years later. Today the Caribbean is the holiday playground that Bill Butlin visualised. Unfortunately his pioneering venture was just a few years ahead of its time.

The city financiers lost confidence in him and for seven years Bill Butlin felt it was tactful to keep away. He held his annual general meetings on the camps and invited the shareholders to stay for three days, as well as giving them a free bottle of whisky and gin. But by 1960 he was back in favour with The Stock Exchange and to mark the occasion he held his annual general meeting in central London, draping the walls of Winchester House with multi-coloured shields of the six camps and photographs of happy holidaymakers. To celebrate the occasion he gave each one of the 500 shareholders who attended the meeting a gift of a small white plaster bust of himself.

Bill on the move. Above, his 1930s Delahaye car; below, one of his six 'Busy Be[e]' aircraft; right, vintage car with Kay Bury & band leader Eric Winstone.

'After the war Butlin's was the place everyone talked about, if you went there you were a millionaire. If you had Butlin's luggage labels everyone would stare at you on the train.'

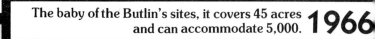

The baby of the Butlin's sites, it covers 45 acres and can accommodate 5,000. **1966**

Bu t

BARRY

PLAYHOUSE

QUIET LO

land

SLAND

When Butlin's first opened competitions were a popular weekly event, as they are today, and all the campers were encouraged to take part and enter into the fun of them. In 1937 there was a driving competition and one of the competitors was Frank Watson, in his Standard 8 car. All the drivers were blindfolded and had to drive around rubber bollards directed by their passenger. Frank's wife, Annie, put her head out of the car sun roof and called out instructions, but Frank knocked all the bollards over, and they didn't win.

Annie won cups for winning the high dive and the long plunge. In the mouth organ competition she won some talcum powder, other prizes were two seats reserved in the dance hall for the week.

Campers would sit making costumes for the fancy dress competition, and the men would roll up their trouser legs for the Knobbly Knees, which in 1948, was judged by Laurel and Hardy. There was a crocheting competition, where campers had to sit outside and crochet a lace edging. In the 1950s there were Princess Elizabeth and Marilyn Monroe Look Alike Competitions. Campers could enter a Snorer of the Week competition, one to find the Shiniest Bald Head and the Shaver Of The Week, which was sponsored by Philishave, the makers of electric razors. Every morning contestants had to go to a shop on the camp where there was a Philishave counter. They were loaned a razor and they had to stand there and shave. The contents of the razor were then emptied into an envelope and at the end of the week, the winner was the man with the most beard shavings.

A lot of the Butlin's competitions were sponsored by national newspapers, and other large companies. Rizla sponsored the Cigarette Rolling competition, and Lux soap sponsored one for the loveliest complexion.

Since 1961 Mrs Cooper's children have entered so many competitions that they have won 34 free Butlin's holidays.

BONNY BABY

A Butlin Holiday Picture

Baby, you're a winner

The weekly Bonny Baby competitions started after the war are very popular. There are categories with ages ranging from nought to three years old. Babies sat

EVERYONE'S A WINNER!

on their mothers' knee, were judged by the vicar, the head of the nursery and a camp committee member. During the 1960s it was sponsored by Nursery World and in the 1970s by Gerba.

Today it is sponsored by Milupa who give the winners a teddy bear. A Redcoat, sucking a large dummy and wearing a huge nappy, a safety pin and a hairy chest used to join in the line-up of competitors.

99

Guess Who?

There was a shop on the camp which hired out fancy dress costumes, crinolines and cowboy outfits, for campers who weren't able to make their own. But for a lot of people, part of the holiday was to sit sewing costumes, or adapting what ever was at hand: newspapers, polythene bags and waste paper baskets. Sometimes the costumes had a topical theme, like the camper who won in 1939 dressed up as Hitler.

Below, Pre-war Pearly Queen at Skegness. Right, Fleet St hackette, Victor Bonutto & Bognor dustman. Far right, 1984 Christmas Fancy Dress, Mary Merril & Margaret Wilson as Skegness Tramps. Below, Victor Bonutto at the Barry Island end-of-season chain-saw massacre.

Butlin's Holiday Camp, Skegness.

100

Two Tired Beauty Queens

Margaret Wilson first went to Butlin's in 1937 when she was fifteen. Her father lost his false teeth on one of the amusement rides. Margaret returned to Butlin's in 1947, when there were competitions in the dining room for the best laid table and the quickest service. Twenty years ago she met Mary Merril who was also from Sheffield, and they have both been going to Butlin's with their families ever since. For the last eight years they have entered the weekly fancy dress competition as a double act, and every year they have won. Five years ago Mary started writing songs to go with their costumes. These have ranged from the 'Daughters of Mama Cass' to 'Toot and Ploot', the two characters with green faces who were in a Butlin's advertising campaign. When Mary and Margaret went to the Butlin's hotel in Spain, they dressed up and sang about two tired-out beauty queens. In 1985 they came first with a song which Margaret wrote, 'We're Two Skegness Tramps', both of them wearing matching black cardboard bowler hats and spats with trousers and waistcoats tied up with string. For Butlin's 50th Anniversary Mary Merril has written a song:

(To the tune of 'I Do Like to be Beside the Seaside')

'Oh I do like to go and stay at Butlin's,
At home abroad where ever it may be,
The style has changed we know,
From what we called the good old
days,
But still it can't be beaten in oh so
many ways.
You can't beat the fun from all the
Redcoats,
Their ingenuity has really to be seen
From judging beauty queens
Or would-be stars it seems
They are always on the go.
And in conclusion may we have a guess,
The age of all this effort and success,
We'll add it up you know

101

Butlin it!

Show Your Talent at Butlin's

Helen Shapiro went to the Butlin's Hotel at Brighton with her parents in 1959 when she was thirteen. At meal times she remembers having different coloured soups that all tasted the same, and eating bacon for the first time. She wore her white stiletto winkle-picker shoes, learned to roller skate and fancied a dark-eyed boy who was a Redcoat. She entered the talent competition, singing 'The Birth Of The Blues' and came second and said, 'I was nervous and the audience was very big.

In 1982 she sang at Barry Island, in the Butlin's '60s Weekend'.

Butlin's Gave Me Bottle!

Mike Reid took his wife and two small children on holiday. They drove down to Minehead, past the Butlin's camp and decided to stay. There were several competitions, and Mike felt that he was a professional and they were all amateurs. But his wife persuaded him to enter the talent competition, and he got through to the area finals, then the semi-finals and eventually to the finals at the London Palladium.

Cyril Fletcher ran the talent competitions at the camp and gave Mike strict instructions: he wasn't to use any bad language, or tell any jokes that were even slightly blue, and his act mustn't go over three minutes. He opened his act with a joke about an advertisement in a newspaper: 'Woman deaf in left ear, wearing hearing aid, would like to meet man deaf in right ear, also wearing hearing aid. Object: stereo'.

When he got to the finals at the London Palladium, he only came second in the competition. Although he didn't win, Mike decided that if he could beat all the other contestants over a period of twenty-two weeks at each camp, he must have something that was a little bit different.

102

The Ladder Of Fame . . . I Want To Be An Actor . . . Gracious Lady . . . Super Cook . . . Brain of the Week . . . Father & Son

At about the same time the television programme, *The Comedians* was just starting and the producer was looking for artists. Mike telephoned Granada Television, and told the programme producer and was given an audition. 'If I hadn't been to Butlin's, and performed in front of all those hundreds of people, I don't think I would ever have had the confidence to ring a television producer,' he says looking back on the experience.

Today Mike often performs at Butlin's Midnight Cabaret, where children aren't allowed, which means he can tell slightly risqué jokes.

Butlin's Bathing Beauties

Beauty competitions started at Butlin's when it opened. The first year one was judged by the Lancashire Cotton Queen, and in 1938 by Gracie Fields, who gave the winner a powder compact. In 1955 the competition was called the Holiday Princess, after the two Royal Princesses Elizabeth and Margaret, and was very popular among the campers, who put on their swim suits whatever the weather. The finals were held at the Royal Albert Hall. In 1960 it was sponsored by the Sunday newspaper the *Empire News* and the winning prize was £1,000.

In 1984 the winner of the finals received £2,500 and two weeks' holiday in Europe, as well as a replica of the trophy that is valued at £12,000. For the last five years the winner has automatically become the pin up for the Royal Marines, attending regimental functions all over the world.

Right, After dinner prospective beauty queens observed the effect on the Giant Weigher.

104

Silver Rose Bowl Challenge Trophy

In 1954 the magazine *Vanity Fair* sponsored a competition at Butlin's under their own name, which was taken over a year later by *She* magazine, who sponsored it for the next 30 years. The competitors could be aged from 15 to 50 and had to show charm, fashion sense, confidence and personality. The heats were weekly and the semi-finals were held at one of the Butlin's Hotels. The grand finals were at the Royal Albert Hall. The winner of the first competition in 1956 was Sheila Manners who received £50 plus a 'top-to-toe outfit', an offer of a contract on the Butlin's entertainment staff for the season, and she was allowed to keep the Silver Rose Bowl trophy for a year. Second prize was £30 and the third prize was £20. The judges were Ronald Shiner, Patrick Barr, Nancy Spain and editor Joan Werner Laurie.

As the years went by there were so many competitors that the semi-finals had to be split, and one was held in the north of England and one in the south. In 1984, *She* magazine stopped sponsoring the competition and Ultra Glow took it over it is now called Miss Ultra Glow, but the competitors still have to have the same charm and dress sense.

There is a weekly competition for Miss Evening Wear which is sponsored by Goldwells, the makers of bottled snowball cocktails and for girls aged between fourteen and eighteen, there is The Miss Mod. Competition.

The 60s

The 80s

The 50s
The 70s

The Most Glamorous Grandmother

In 1955 Bill Butlin was on a visit to America where he met Marlene Dietrich, whom he thought was the most glamorous grandmother he had ever seen. When he returned home he decided that Butlin's should hold a weekly Glamorous Grandmother competition, with the finals at the end of the season. The early competitions were sponsored by newspapers.

Seventeen Times a Finalist

Frances Maloney has been competing in the Glamorous Grandmother competition for 25 years, longer than any other competitor, but she has never won. Seventeen times she has reached the grand finals, and every time she has been one of the seven runners up. So far the nearest she has ever got to winning was in 1984 when she received £500 for coming third.

Frances first went to Butlin's with her family and grandson in 1961. She watched the competitions and decided she could do better. She put some blue flowers in her hair, wore her best little black dress and entered the Glamorous Grandmothers. To her surprise she won. Since then she has not missed a year.

Frances says that the Glamorous Grandmother Competition is now her life. It has given her the confidence to do photographic modelling, radio broadcasts and newspaper interviews giving hair and beauty tips. She designs her own clothes for the finals, even going to the trouble of finding out the colour of the wallpaper, so that her clothes won't clash. She takes four pairs of tights and two lipsticks with her, and her own hairdresser. The finals are judged every year by different personalities and Frances has met them all, from Norman Hartnell to Joe Bugner. Since she first started competing, she has watched Glamorous Grandmothers getting younger every year. At last year's finals Frances, at 69, was the oldest competitor, the youngest was 34, but despite that she intends to carry on.

23 Times a Semi-Finalist

Since 1962 Alice Mathews has entered the weekly heats of the Glamorous Grandmother competition 23 times, and every time she has got through to the semi finals. Three times she has been in the grand finals, but she has never won or been

placed in the last four. For winning the weekly heats she has received leather hand bags, evening clutch bags, a set of carving knives, a dressing table set, string of pearls and holiday holdalls. At 76, she no longer enters the competition to win. She says that now she just enjoys being there. Her year is spent looking in shops and magazines, planning what to wear that is different.

In 1981 she crocheted her own dress.

The competition has made her famous in her home town of Leeds. Alice has made several radio broadcasts, and appeared in the local newspaper. In 1984 she paid £48, the most she has ever spent, for a dress for the competition. The cheapest one cost £5, fifteen years ago. A lot of people bet on the finals of the Glamorous Grandmother comptition, and the odds are published in a London newspaper. Last year Alice was 33 to 1.

Far left: Frances Maloney wearing a dress made from a stole for the area finals 1965.
Left: Frances Maloney the oldest competitor with the winner, Julie Kesby, Bognor 1985.
Above: The finals 1981. Alice Mathews at 73 with the youngest contestant, aged 36.

Alice Mathews — Supergran!

1962

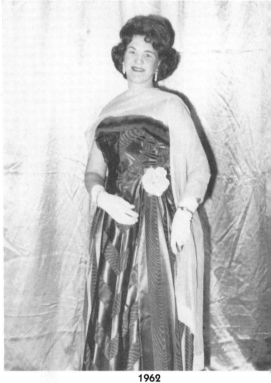

1962

1980

1981

1969

1970

1982

1983

Glamorous Grandmother – just in time!

Helped by Castor Oil!

At one of the Glamorous Grandmother Competitions, a contestant wasn't quite a bona fide grandmother. Although her daughter's baby was due any day, it hadn't actually arrived. As the date of the competition grew closer, panic set in, and the would-be grandmother spooned castor oil down her daughter, and on the day of the competition, the baby was born.

The competition now has over 10,000 entries every season. Two hundred are chosen to attend the finals, one in the south of England and one in the north. In 1985 the oldest finalist was ninety-two and the youngest was thirty-five.

1979

The Judges are:

ANITA HARRIS
Well known British recording star

DIANA MORAN
Television's famous Green Goddess

DOROTHY HYMAN M.B.E.
British Olympic Gold Medalist

FREDDIE GARRITY
Popular entertainer and recording star with Freddie & The Dreamers

PETER BONETTI
Former Chelsea and England Goalkeeper

JOHN PULMAN
Former World Snooker Champion for 11 years and now a well known snooker commentator
Prizes will be presented by **Mr. R. L. Webb**
Managing Director of Butlin's Holidays

Welcome to the Butlin's Most Glamorous
If you turn to the back page, you'll find a replica of the judges score

1. JOYCE WHITFIELD
WALLASEY

2. JENNIFER WILLIAMS
CARDIFF

7. BARBARA CHETHAM
SALE

8. MARY PEPLOW
BROMSGROVE

9. SUE BROWN
LEICESTER

10. MAUREEN SCOTT
DEWSBURY

15. SALLY McCANDLESS
LONDONDERRY

16. DORIS WILSON
LANCASTER

17. JULIE KESBY
SOUTHAMPTON

18. FRANCES MALONEY
LEIGH

GLAMOROUS GRANDMOTHER

Butlin's

The 1984 Grand Final

Reigning Champion 1983 PATRICIA MITCHELL from Plymouth.

1959

Butlin's MOST GLAMOROUS GRANDMOTHER OF GREAT BRITAIN

1984

...other of Great Britain 1984. Grand Finals.

...you agree with the judges!) We hope you have an enjoyable afternoon.

3. MARGARET BOYD
DARWEN

4. MAVIS COLLINSON
HULL

5. JANE COLLYER
WOKINGHAM

6. PATRICIA PROBERT
STOURPORT ON SEVERN

11. EDNA JONES
SHEERNESS

12. SYLVIA JACKSON
BOLTON

13. AUDREY WHITE
FORFAR

14. JOAN SHAW
LYTHAM ST ANNES

19. ANN STARKEY
SEVENOAKS

20. MAUREEN WORLOCK
BRISTOL

And the prizes !

1st: £2,500 cash plus
a Wings Faraway Holiday
to the SEYCHELLES
2nd: £750
3rd: £500
6 Runners-up £200 each and £100
each for the remaining
finalists.

Knees Up!

The weekly Knobbly Knees competition started at Butlin's before the war, and fifty years and many thousands of knees later it is still going strong. In 1959 when the comedian Ted Rogers was a Redcoat, one of his jobs was to organise the Knobbly Knees competition. In order to encourage campers to join in the fun and roll up their trouser legs, he used to tape ping pong balls to his knees.

116

Interval for laughter during rehearsals. Billy Ternent, Frankie Howerd and Jimmie James do a " Knobbly Knees" for the benefit of Billy Butlin.

LOVELY LEGS

Some of the Butlin's competitions have big money prizes, such as Miss Lovely Legs, sponsored by Pretty Polly. The first prize is £1,000 and a faraway holiday, the second prize is £500 and the third prize is £250.

118

Below, Knobbly Knees prize awarded by Laurel & Hardy, 1948.

Come Dancing

In 1947 Butlin's ran the first National Valeta Competition which was judged by the resident dancing instructor on each camp. The finals were held at the Royal Albert Hall, where the floor would be packed with a thousand dancers. Butlin's now hold the largest dance festivals in the world with competitors coming from as far away as Russia, Australia, Finland, and Africa. There are annual dance and music festivals for Old Tyme, Modern, Latin American and Ballroom, as well as square dancing, morris dancing, rock 'n' roll, disco free style, folk dancing, highland dancing and majorettes. At the camp at Mosney in Ireland there used to be Ceili-dancing. In 1985 there were 70,000 entries at all the Butlin's dance and music festivals and in 1986, with two additional festivals, 100,000 are expected.

LATIN

HIGHLAND

LEISURE SEPTEMBER 12, 1966

1 Frank and Phyllis Westbrook (London); 2 Thomas and Mary Kelley (Stoke on Trent); 3 Steve Wright, Kathy Keeган (Darlington)
FORMATION TROPHY
1 Blackpool Team (D & G. Stead)

RUSSIANS WIN AT CLACTO

A SENSATIONAL turn of events brought dancers at Clacton holiday camp to their toes when the winners of the News of the World novice trophy were announced. The sensation was a win by a Russian couple, Chevslovas and Jurate Norviasha.

It is the first time that a Soviet couple has won a ball-room event of any kind in this country.

Second were Leonard and Margaret Page, of Harrow, and third Allan and Maureen Ford, of Stoke-on-Trent.

Winners of the Butlin pre-Championship Trophy were Philip Conway and Jacqueline of Sheffield, followed by Kevin Richardson, Virginia Hollingshead, of Bristol.

In the eight couple formation event Stan Jac North Twenty Latin Team, from Barnet, Herts Frank and Peggy Spencer's Modern Team, Penge, South London, into second place Norma Graves' Modern Team, from Wa Cheshire, in third place.
More details next week.

Baby, Let's Dance?

Every year Butlin's hold young and juvenile ballroom dance festivals for ages ranging from the under-fives to the over thirty-fives. One of the youngest ballroom dancing competitors was four years' old, and the oldest was over eighty. Butlin's hold the British and World Ballet Tap and Modern Dance Championships every year on one of the camps, with dancers aged from ten to seventeen. In the highland dance festival there is a section for the under-fives, the youngest competitor was three-and-a-half years old.

TEAM

BALLET

O'BURNS

DISCO

OLD TYME

Take your partners

When the war was over, people were eager to dance to big bands in big ballrooms. Butlin's was able to provide both. Jack and Joyce Briggs were amateur dancers who won the Old Tyme dancing at the first Butlin's Dance Festival at Filey in 1951. They took their six-week old daughter, Jackalyn with them, and by the time she was eight she too was dancing at a Butlin's festival. During the 1950s the first prize at the dance festivals was a £50 voucher, which could be spent either on or off the camp. Jack and Joyce Briggs won two vouchers and five free holidays, as well as numerous trophies. In 1955 they turned professional and over the next ten years they won six cash prizes of £80 each, and their daughter Jacqueline, who followed in their dancing footsteps, has won Butlin's vouchers worth hundreds of pounds. In the 1960s Butlin's forbade professional dancers to take part. Today the competitors are all amateurs. Jack and Joyce Briggs are now judges at Butlin's dance festivals.

Jack and Joyce Briggs Official Board winners, Filey 1956

Right, Jack and Joyce Briggs formation team winners at Royal Albert Hall reunion 1967

Jackalyn Briggs age 3 with her father dancing at Filey 1954.

Jackalyn Briggs entering the Butlin's Latin American competition 1967

Odds on a Donkey

Don Trapnell owns donkeys who give rides on the beach. In the 1950s he went on holiday to Butlin's with his family, and slipped into the suggestion box the idea of having donkey derbys and donkey rides on the camps, but he didn't receive a reply. The following year he wrote to the eight camp entertainment managers, who sent his letters to the head office. Butlin's decided to experiment by letting Don hold one donkey derby at the Minehead camp. The idea caught on so quickly that the two shilling tote tickets and programmes sold out in one day, four days before the race. Butlin's decided that they should hold weekly donkey derbys and give donkey rides on all the camps. Don Trapnell still works with his donkeys on four of the Butlin's sites. One of the largest amounts to be won on the weekly donkey derby was £1,249, 35 pence.

Camp Mayor wins donkey derby.

Refuelling at Skegness.

Mrs M Arkwright holding her donkey derby winning cheque for £1,248, 35 pence in August 1984.

Butlin's Beauty and the Beast

There were always plenty of competitions at Butlin's which gave women the chance to look beautiful, ranging from the Junior Miss to the Holiday Princess and the Glamorous Grandmother. In the 1950s there was the Marilyn Monroe Look-alike Competition and the Loveliest Complexion, sponsored by Lux. While the women were trying to look beautiful, the men pulled Ugly Faces or showed off their Knobbly Knees.

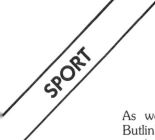

Come on, be a sport!

As well as the morning Keep Fit, All Butlin's campers were encouraged to join in the weekly team inter-house sports. There were the regular events such as netball, football, snooker and water sports, and there were the less conventional ones, such as egg-and-spoon, leap frog, tug-of-war and carpet racing, when a woman sat on a rug while a man dragged her round the rather messy donkey derby course.

THE BOXING INSTRUCTOR

Hello Campers !

"I saw Stars, I heard the Angels sing."

This will not be YOUR Signature Tune, if you will let me initiate you into the secrets of the noble art.

Speaking of tunes, and to avoid disappointment, please note that I am not a crooner, and the following is my first (and last) attempt at verse :—

If YOU are a novice, I'll teach you to spar
  Without any scoffing or jeers,
And you won't see a star or get one little scar,
  Nor go home with cauliflower ears.

But if you're a Pro., we'll have a real go,
For maybe you're better than I.
  And won't the lads shout
  If you knock ME about !
So come on, old chap, have a try !

1120

2775

1870

329

4573

BUTLIN'S SKEGNESS HOLIDAY CAMP.

WRESTLING!

BUTLINS
HOLIDAY
CAMP,
SKEGNESS

2112

33

Telephone :—Skegness **372**.

Telegrams :—Amuse, Skegness.

Our Ref......HEC/AB.

Your Ref.....................

REG. OFFICES :—THE NEW AMUSEMENT PARK,

GRAND PARADE, SKEGNESS.

18th November 193

Top: Butlin's company letter heading in the 1920s. Originally the slogan was on the side of his fairground organ.

Bottom: Bill Butlin first introduced dodgems on his Skegness site in 1928, a few months later he acquired the sole agency for selling them in Europe.

21 CLUBS
Top: V.E. Day at Filey camp, 1946.
Bottom: Souvenir programme
21 Club Leave Centre, Blankenberghe 1945.

Bill Butlin set up the 21 Clubs throughout Europe. They offered food, dancing and entertainment. He was one of the first civilians to have landed in France after D-Day, to organise leave centres.

BLANKENBERGHE
LEAVE CENTRE
1945

SOUVENIER ENTERTAINMENT
SUPPLEMENT

ISSUED BY ARMY WELFARE SERVICES

A WONDERFUL AERIAL VIEW OF
BUTLIN'S LUXURY HOLIDAY CAMP
S K E G N E S S

A pre-war Skegness holiday brochure.

Where *your* comfort is *our* concern...

JOVIAL JOE.

RAPIDLY becoming one of the most famous figures in the country is jovial Joe Velich, our principal chef, on the left. Below you see him busy in one of the kitchens, and then visiting the restaurants to make sure that everyone is well satisfied. Right, part of the interior of a chalet, showing the view across one of the lawns. All very pleasant, isn't it?

A TYPICAL DAY'S FARE :
Breakfast : Grapefruit, bacon and eggs, bread and butter, marmalade, tea. Lunch : Roast leg of lamb, mint sauce, beans, roast and boiled potatoes, fruit tart and custard, bread and butter.

AND THEN FOR TEA : Brown and white bread and butter, jam, cakes. Dinner : Soup, steamed salmon and cucumber, blancmange, cheese.

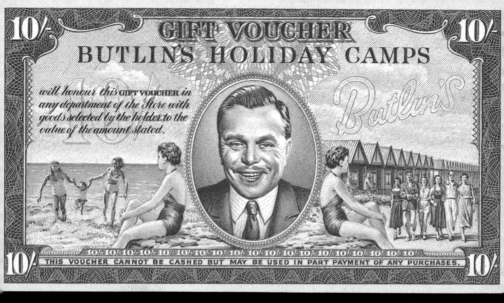

GIFT VOUCHER

BUTLIN'S HOLIDAY CAMPS

will honour this GIFT VOUCHER in any department of the Store with goods selected by the holder to the value of the amount stated.

Butlin's

10/- 10/- 10/- 10/- 10/- 10/- 10/- 10/- 10/- 10/- 10/- 10/- 10/- 10/- 10/- 10/- 10/-

THIS VOUCHER CANNOT BE CASHED BUT MAY BE USED IN PART PAYMENT OF ANY PURCHASES.

Butlin's Gift Voucher. Prize for winning the tombola.

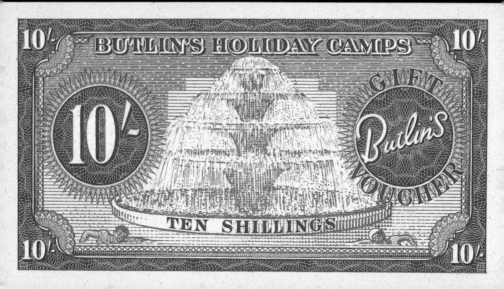

BUTLIN'S HOLIDAY CAMPS

10/-

GIFT

Butlin's

VOUCHER

TEN SHILLINGS

ANNIVERSARY

Butlin's first reunion was held at the Royal Albert Hall in 1946. It was attended by HRH the Duke of Edinburgh. Later the shows went on for five nights. 40,000 campers attended during the week. The entertainers who had performed at Butlin's were there. The finals of the competitions were held. The last Butlin's reunion was in 1966.

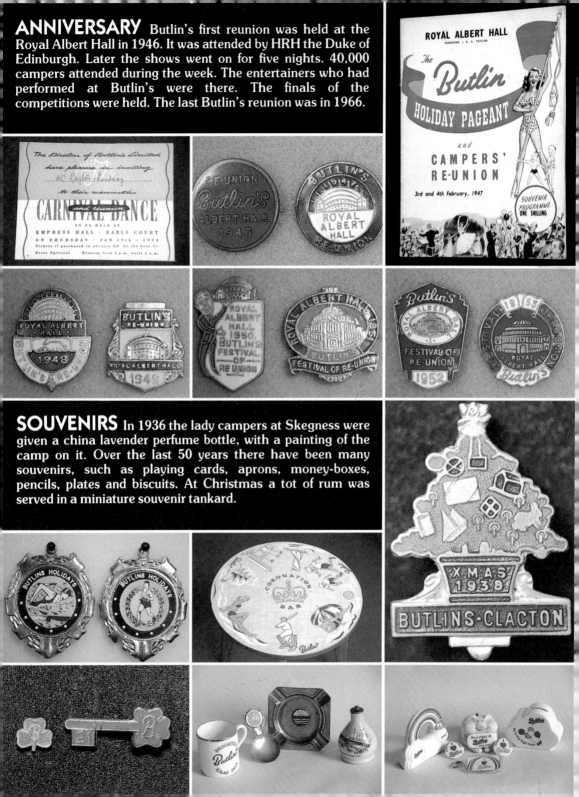

ROYAL ALBERT HALL

MANAGER — C. S. TAYLOR

The *Butlin* HOLIDAY PAGEANT and CAMPERS' RE-UNION

3rd and 4th February, 1947

SOUVENIR PROGRAMME. ONE SHILLING

SOUVENIRS

In 1936 the lady campers at Skegness were given a china lavender perfume bottle, with a painting of the camp on it. Over the last 50 years there have been many souvenirs, such as playing cards, aprons, money-boxes, pencils, plates and biscuits. At Christmas a tot of rum was served in a miniature souvenir tankard.

AT YOUR SERVICE There were about 100 Redcoats on each camp who organised all the interhouse games and competitions. Now there are about 30. In 1984 at the six Butlin's centres the staff cooked and served 97,000 dozen eggs (no one is ever given a broken one), 600 tons of chips and 7 million pints of beer.

CLUBS

The Butlin Beaver club for young children started in 1951. It was going to be called the Busy Bee Club, but there was already one in existence. At one time there were 200,000 Beavers. The 913 Club was for children aged between 9 and 13. When they grew up they could join the Harvey Club, Butlin's Social clubs, or the Car and Motor Cycle Club.

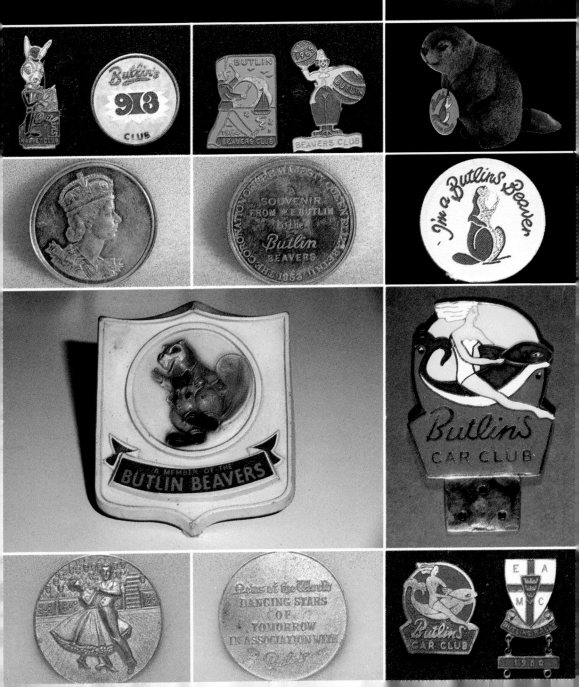

If you're a Butlin Beaver you're a friend of mine

The Butlin Beaver Club was started in 1951 for campers' children who were under nine years old. Ciaran Jesson was a registered Butlin Beaver when he was only 36 hours old.

Originally it was going to be called The Busy Bee Club but unfortunately there already was one. Frank Mansell came up with another name, still with the same B.B. initials, the Butlin's Beavers. Beaver was Lord Beaverbrook's nickname during the war and he and Bill Butlin worked together and became firm friends, which could have been where the name came from.

There was a grand initiation ceremony for new Beavers which was performed at the Beaver Lodge by the Camp Mayor wearing his ceremonial robes and brass chain. Membership was for life and Beavers received a badge, a Beaver money bank and birthday and Christmas cards signed by King Beaver.

Almost as soon as the club was started it had 200,000 members and a programme on Radio Luxembourg, presented by 'Uncle' Eric Winston, the band leader. The club had its own code of conduct which members had to promise to abide by and on each camp there were Beaver Lodges, where they held meetings.

Butlin's BEAVER CLUB RULES

1. **B**e kind to dumb animals.
2. **E**ager always to help others.
3. **A**im to be clean, neat and tidy.
4. **V**ictory by Fair Play.
5. **E**nergetic at work and play.
6. **R**espect for parents and all elders.

and in all things
BE AS EAGER AS A BEAVER

Members: 3–8 years inclusive.

THE BEAVERS' SONG

Sing to the tune of
"We're All Friends Here"

If you're a Butlin Beaver you're a friend of mine,
If you've the Beaver Spirit then the world is fine,
In our lodge you'll find good company,
To be a Butlin Beaver is great fun you'll soon agree.
We are the eager Beavers and we promise true,
To keep the golden rule in everything we do.
Come and join us – wear a badge – learn the secret sign,
Be an Eager Beaver – Busy Eager Beaver –
If you're a Butlin Beaver you're a friend of mine.

★

Butlin's Clubs

Beaver Club	Cycling Club	Melf Club
913 Club	Old Tyme Club	Harvey Club
15 Club	Grand Bahamas Club	Choral Society
Motor Cycle Club	21 Club	Photographic Society
Car Club	Social Club	

Just a song at Butlin's

Verse:—

Leave your shop or fac-to-ry, your of-fice or your home;

Sing-along

The Butlin's Choral Society was started in the early 1950s, and with more or less the same people, it lasted for thirteen years. All the members were Butlin's campers. Albert Brown and his wife sang in the choral society at Billy Graham meetings and in Birmingham Cathedral, for charity at the Coliseum and New Victoria Theatre in London and at about sixty other functions during the year. At weekends they would travel to one of the camps and sing in the Sunday night cabaret. They made several records of Christmas carols and Butlin songs such as 'Roll Out Of Bed'.

1. GOOD MORNING, CAMPERS

Roll out of bed in the morning
With a great big smile and a good, good
    morning.
Wake up with a grin,
There's a new day a-tumbling in.
Wake with the sun and the rooster;
Cock-a-doodle-do like the rooster useta.
You'll find it worth while
If you roll out of bed with a smile.

Do your singing in the Chalet
As you start this happy day.
While you're singing in the Chalet
Think of all the fun you'll get the Butlin
    way.

Coffee and rolls with your honey
Turns a gloomy day to a day that's sunny
You'll find it worth while
If you roll out of bed with a smile.

2. A HOLIDAY AT BUTLIN'S

Well, here we are
From near and far,
A Holiday at Butlin's;
We swim and dance
And find Romance,
A Holiday at Butlin's;
The Friendships made
Will never fade,
A Holiday at Butlin's;
We'll meet again
We all know when,
Next Holiday at Butlin's.
Well, sing this song
You can't go wrong,
A Holiday at Butlin's;
To lose the blues
Just spread the news,
A Holiday at Butlin's;

We won't forget
The friends we met,
On Holiday at Butlin's;
And through the years
The thought that cheers,
A Holiday at Butlin's.

3. BUTLIN BUDDIES

Leave your shop and factory
Leave our office and your home,
Come and spend a Holiday beside the
    briny foam.
Come on all you Scholars, come and put
    away your studies
Come and join the happy band that's
    known as Butlin Buddies.

Hi-yah fellas we are Butlin's buddies,
Now that summer's come again and life
    is gay
What shall we do with a face that's long
We'll teach it the words of the Butlin
    Song,
With a Hip-Hip-Hip-Pip Hooray
Yes we have joined the happy band of
    Butlin Buddies,
And we're all together on our holiday,
Other folks have other ways of digging in
    the sand,
It's being Butlin Buddies beats the band.

The Butlin's Choral Society outside the Skegness theatre.

Come and join the hap-py band that's known as BUTLIN BUDDIES.

4. BUTLIN'S WALTZ

All good things come to an end they say,
This we know is true,
And so before we go on our way,
There is one thing still to do.

It's time to dance the Butlin Waltz
It's time to say good-night.
It's time for sweet and pleasant dreams
Until the morning light,
So go to bed each sleepy head
And as we dream we'll say,
Thank you Mr. Butlin for a very happy
 day.

5. TRAMP TRAMP TRAMP

Some come from the highland, some
 come from the low,
Jogging along hearty and strong merrily
 we go.
Swinging thro' the byway, thro' the
 country lane,

        Refrain

Now all together let it go again:
Tramp, tramp, tramp, tramp here we
 come—
Jolly good campers every one.
Tramp, tramp, tramp, tramp hear the call

Hi-de-hi! Hi-de-ho!
We all came down to Butlin's, Butlin's by
 the sea.
Now we're all as happy, as happy as can
 be,
Tramp, tramp, tramp, tramp hear the
 call—
Hi-de-hi! Hi-de-ho!

6. HI-DE-HI

Hi-de-hi, hi-de-ho; hi-de-hi, hi-de-ho,
When things are looking gloomy,
And skies are dull and grey,
Remember that the sun will come and
 shine another day,
So open up your faces wide,
And let me hear you say,
Hi-de-hi, hi-de-ho.

7. NOW WE'RE AT BUTLIN'S

We're going to spend a holiday
We've worked and saved all year,
We've put our worries on the shelf,
We haven't got a care,
We caught a train an early one
To —— by the sea,
And now we're here at Butlin's

That's the place for you and me.
Now we're at Butlin's,
Jolly old Butlin's
That's the place to make you gay,
Where you're happy ev'ry day,
Yes here at Butlin's,
Jolly old Butlin's,
Is ev'rybody happy hear us roar,
YES! Forget your little worries
While you're basking in the sun
And when the sun has gone to bed
There is always lots of fun
While you're at Butlin's,
Jolly old Butlin's,
That's the holiday that's well worth
 waiting for.
Ta-ra-ra, B-U-T-L-I-N-S
And we know we'll soon be back again
 for more,
Ta-ra-ra B-U-T-L-I-N-S
Butlin's for ever more.

8. AT A HOLIDAY CAMP

There was I 'neath a starry sky,
It was a heavenly night,
We met and then we met again,
It was love at first sight.

AT A HOLIDAY CAMP I found a lovely
 romance,
AT A HOLIDAY CAMP one summer's day.
Her tiny chalet was just next door but
 two.
When she said "Hello" then my heart
 said:
"Oh, here's the girl for you."

AT A HOLIDAY CAMP it's so romantic
Moonlit nights are simply made for
 two—
Soon she'll be Missus
And this is where we'll spend our
 honeymoon,
AT A HOLIDAY CAMP where dreams
 come true.

9. GOOD-NIGHT, CAMPERS

Good-night, Campers, I can see you
 yawning,
Good-night, Campers, see you in the
 morning,
You must cheer up or you'll soon be
 dead,
For I've heard it said,
Folks die in bed,
So we'll say good-night, Campers,
 don't sleep in your braces;
Good-night, Campers, put your
 teeth in Jeyes;
Drown your sorrow, bring the
 bottles back to-morrow
Good-night, Campers, good-night.

'Broken down have we?'

Campers Service, 1955.

BENEFITS OF MEMBERSHIP

(*a*) All Butlin Camps now have motorized patrols to render assistance to Club members.

(*b*) The driver of any motor car, motor cycle or 3-wheeled vehicle displaying the badge will be entitled to half price admission to any Butlin Camp as a Day Visitor (passengers to pay full price). Club Members may enjoy all the Sporting and Entertainment facilities available to Day Visitors.

(*c*) During the period of their holiday, two half-day tours to places of interest in the locality of the Holiday Camps at which they are staying will be organised for the benefit of members and without charge. The tours will be led by a Butlin Motor Cycle Scout.

(*d*) Two Motor Car Competitions and one Motor Cycle Competition will be organised each week at all Holiday Camps. Cups and prizes will be presented for each event.

(*e*) Two Butlin Motor Cycle Scouts in distinctive uniform will be resident at each Holiday Camp for the purpose of giving advice and assistance as may be required by Club Members. They will also carry out emergency repairs at appropriate repayments on all vehicles which carry the Club badge.

(*f*) Butlin Motor Cycle Scouts will also patrol the main roads leading to Butlin Holiday Camps on the days which holiday-makers arrive and depart. They will assist Club members in trouble and give advice on directions and routes.

'Hello again!'

Above, HRH The Duke of Edinburgh with Mr W E Butlin, MBE walking through a Redcoat guard of honour at the Royal Albert Hall. Right, trick cyclists in the cabaret.

Campers' reunion

The Butlin's Social Clubs and the Albert Hall reunions were the brain-child of Colonel Basil Brown. The idea was to encourage campers to keep in touch with one another during the winter when the camps were closed.

Butlin's Social Clubs opened up all over the country in areas where almost everyone in the whole town had been on holiday at Butlin's. Campers got together, with the help of a visiting Redcoat and held weekly meetings and an annual dance.

The first nationwide reunion of Butlin's campers was held at the Royal Albert Hall in 1946 for just one night. The star was Evelyn Laye. It was so successful that the following year it was extended for three days and after that, until 1966, when they stopped, the shows went on every night for a week. They started on Tuesday and finished on Saturday, when there would be an extra show in the afternoon for children.

Every night 5,000 campers, 40,000 in a week, would be entertained by the stars that they had seen at Butlin's. As well as the Butlin's Choral Society, the Butlin's Keep Fit Team and military bands giving displays,

Hundreds dance

there would be cabaret acts and the finals of all the major competitions. Campers would take to the floor in their hundreds and dance to the music of various forty-piece bands, as well as meeting their favourite Redcoats.

Campers paid a small entrance fee but the 250 people who had all sat on the weekly campers' committees during the season were given free seats. The Duke of Edinburgh would attend and receive a cheque for the Playing Fields Association. The year that he was unable to, Sir Laurence Olivier took his place.

Kay Bury, the Chief Redcoat Hostess, looked after Bill Butlin's special guests at the Albert Hall and presented bouquets to all the stars. She chaperoned the contestants for the Holiday Princess and Glamorous Grandmothers competitions, who were never allowed to go anywhere on their own. Kay had to make sure that they got to the rehearsals and knew which were their dressing rooms. In their time off she took them sightseeing round London.

Sports personalities, singing stars, comedians, actors and actresses, in fact anyone who had performed at Butlin's, would file across the floor of the Albert Hall, fifty at a time, waving to the enthusiastic audience.

At midnight the balloons were released, the National Anthem was played, the souvenir programmes and badges were collected to take home. People renewed holiday friendships, swapped addresses and promised to meet the following summer at Butlin's.

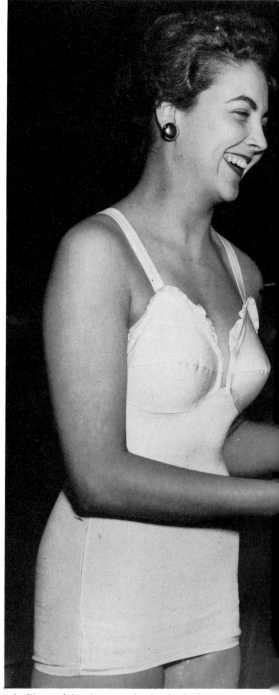

Left, Climax of the demonstration by the Butlin young ladies Keep Fit in Rhythm — a formation of ER in Coronation year.

Bill Butlin planned the strategy of reunions around a table once owned by Ribbentrop and bought from the German embassy after the war.

Above, 20-year old Patricia Butler of Cheshire being presented with the 'Holiday Princess of Great Britain' trophy.

Stars You Have Seldom Heard But Seldom Seen

Before the war, the celebrity concerts had been held on a Sunday because the performers worked for less money. These shows were so popular that after the war Bill Butlin decided to restart them. Although he no longer paid performers less for working on a Sunday, Bill Butlin decided to keep the shows on that day, because as the campers arrived on Saturday, Sunday was their first full day on the site and on Monday, they would send their postcards home. With the night before still fresh in their minds they would write, 'guess who I saw last night at Butlin's'.

During the war the radio was the only source of mass entertainment. It produced a new type of celebrity, whose voice was familiar all over the country, whose name was a household word, but whose faces were almost unknown. Bill Butlin decided to bring radio stars to his camps under the banner, 'Voices you've heard, but faces you've never seen'.

IT'S THAT MAN AGAIN
Butlin's
AT
LUXURY HOLIDAY CAMP
FILEY (near Scarborough)
Special Visit of
TOMMY HANDLEY & FULL ITMA COMPANY
In addition to all the Butlin Holiday attractions

BOOK NOW FOR 22–29 SEPT.
For booking forms apply: BUTLINS LTD. ( ) 439, OXFORD ST., LONDON, W.1

OCTOBER HOLIDAY BARGAIN—FILEY CAMP REMAINING OPEN END OF OCTOBER with all attractions in full swing. Inclusive terms £5:0:0 per week

The first of these new stars was Tommy Handley and the cast of the ITMA (It's That Man Again) shows who were at the peak of their popularity. They were followed by other big names such as: Arthur Askey, Peter Brough and his puppet Archie Andrews, Harold Berens (the star of the radio programme, 'Ignorance Is Bliss'), Kenneth Horne and Richard Murdoch, famous for the song 'Much Binding In The

Marsh', the 'Memory Man' Leslie Welch and the 'spiv' comedian, Charlie Chester, 'The nation's chin-up boy', who was known to everyone as 'Cheerful Charlie Chester'. He played at all the Butlin's camps in the big 2,000-seater theatres right through until the mid-1950s.

Whilst the stars were performing at Butlin's, they all stayed on the camp. They slept in the same chalets as the campers, except there was a bottle of champagne and a bunch of flowers to greet them, and they ate in the dining hall at a special table reserved for guests, but they weren't given special food. During the day it was almost impossible for them to walk around the camp without being hounded by autograph hunters, and posing for photographs.

WOT A GEEZER!

Harold
BERENS

Above, 'Cheerful' Charlie Chester greets Bill Butlin. Right, 'Stinker' Murdoch and Kenneth Horne. Below, Arthur 'Busy Bee' Askey broadcasting from Butlin's.

'I'm Sorry I can't stop Talking, I've got the Wife's Teeth in'

Harold Berens, whose famous catch phrase was, 'Wot a geezer!' first performed at Butlin's Skegness camp in 1950, for a fee of £150 for a Sunday concert. If he did another he was paid a third more. He was a big radio star of the day, but he had hardly ever appeared before very large audiences. When he arrived at Butlin's he was frightened out of his life to see an audience of over 2,000, who rustled paper all through the show, ate, and allowed their children to run up and down the aisles.

On stage he wore in his spiv gear, a large kipper tie, a big jacket and a peaked cap with the brim turned back, and opened his act with a few bars from the song, 'Ignorance is Bliss'.

Harold knew that the majority of the audiences were made up of people from factories who were on Wakes Weeks holidays. He went to the trouble of finding out which area of the country they were from, so that he could do the appropriate dialect and geographically adjust the gags, so that the joke, 'If my wife rolls over twice, she's in Birmingham' would be altered to, 'she's in Bradford'.

He was given strict instructions not to

145

'Open the cage!'

make any jokes about the food, and he wasn't allowed to use blue material. A monologue about 'Piddling Pete, who never stopped piddling' was as far as he was allowed to go.

> **I'm walking down the street the other day. There was an old lady walking in front of me, she comes a tumble. Ace, king, queen, jack, on the deck. I'm behind, I want to help her, see, open her handbag, to give her a bit of fresh air. She opened her eyes, she said: 'Where am I?' I said: 'up in London lady, half a crown'**

The comedian Arthur English made his first professional theatre appearance at Butlin's Sunday concerts in 1950. He had been playing at the Windmill Theatre, where the audiences were more interested in the girls than in the gags. He became famous through Radio Band Box and moved on to Butlin's, where he was top of the bill. Tommy Trinder had been there the week previously, and Hughie Green was doing a quiz show on the camp called, 'Double Your Money', which was sponsored by Lucozade.

Just after the war Arthur played the character of a cockney spiv-cum-barrowboy, who could get anything off ration. His catch phrase was 'Open the cage', and he wore a huge kipper tie that almost touched the floor.

He played at all of the Butlin's camps, and was met at Filey one day by a Redcoat with a long cigarette holder, who said, 'Hello, my name is Charlie Drake and I'm in charge of the celebrities and I'm going to look after you'.

At the height of the summer season, Arthur performed in four, one-hour shows. It didn't matter how good the shows were as long as they didn't overrun. If they went two minutes over the hour, there was trouble, because it meant that the theatre bar takings were down.

Above, Tommy Trinder and playmate.

In the theatre, on either side of the stage, there were two huge ornamental plaster horses being ridden by knights in armour. Arthur used to point to them and jokingly comment, 'They're very strict at Butlin's. Two cleaners come every day to clean these because Mr Butlin won't have any dirty knights on his camp'.

Bruce Forsyth, Norman Vaughan, Hugh Lloyd, Frankie Howerd and Benny Hill, who was paid £15 for two shows, were just some of the young comedians who gained their experience appearing at Butlin's Sunday Night Concerts. The campers didn't find Frankie Howerd very amusing, and neither did Bill Butlin, who suggested that he ought to get out of show business and find himself a job.

The silent comedy team, Laurel and Hardy visited the camp at Skegness. They clowned around and judged the Knobbly Knees competition. When Hoppalong Cassidy arrived all the children on the camp turned out to meet him wearing little cowboy hats and jeans.

The singing group, the Bachelors, were the resident musical entertainers on the camp at Mosney in Eire and like Georgie Fame, Helen Shapiro and Dusty Springfield, who also performed at Butlin's, they were all young up-and-coming entertainers.

The Beverly Sisters first appeared at Butlin's when they were seventeen, in the

Below, Arthur English and playmates.

BLUE MATERIAL

May we remind all Artistes that Butlin's cater for Family Audiences and despite the permissive world outside, we intend to maintain our standards.

BLUE MATERIAL IS THEREFORE UNACCEPTABLE AT BUTLIN'S

CHILDREN DON'T UNDERSTAND IT
PARENTS DON'T LIKE IT
AND WE WON'T HAVE IT – AT ANY .....

PLEASE CO-OPERATE

late 1940s. They were with the band leader Eric Winston, and had done several radio broadcasts, but Butlin's was their first professional engagement. Their father travelled with them to Clacton, Skegness and Filey camps, and slept in the next chalet. A year later they appeared at a Butlin's reunion at the Royal Albert Hall, and sang; 'Remember We Met At Butlin's', which Eric Winston had composed specially for Butlin's and the Beverly Sisters.

'It's time to dance the Butlin Waltz, it's time to say goodnight. It's time for sweet and pleasant dreams, until the morning light. So go to bed each sleepy head, and as we dream we'll say, thank you Mr Butlin for a very happy day.'

147

Stairs to the Stars

Bill Butlin was always keen on having big bands on his camps, for the ballrooms and then, later on, for the concert party shows in the theatre. Dancing was very popular at the time and Butlin's, with its huge ballrooms, promoted the idea of campers being able to dance the night away to live music for no extra charge. One of the first bandleaders at Butlin's before the war was Mantovani, who returned for a few weeks in the early 1950s. Charles Amer was another band leader who had worked for Butlin's as an entertainments manager in 1937, and returned after the war as 'Charles Amer and his Butlin's Boys'. He played at Filey for several years, along with band leader, Dick Denny, Ivy Benson and her All Girls Band, The Squadronnaires and Syd Seymour and His Mad Hatters.

Eric Winston and his orchestra started at Butlin's camp at Clacton when it reopened in 1946. He wrote several 'Butlin's numbers', amongst them 'The Butlin's Conga' and 'The Butlin's Waltz', which was a dance specially invented for campers. During the winter, when the camp closed, Eric Winston the band leader, was known as Uncle Eric and presented a programme from Radio Luxembourg for the thousands of children who were members of the Butlin's Beaver Club.

As the Redcoat Revue became more popular it was decided that it ought to have its own orchestra. Al Fried, who had conducted for the chain of Moss Empire Theatres, joined Butlin's to form the first concert orchestra. He conducted the orchestra for the finals of the Butlin's Talent Competitions that were held at the London Palladium, and stayed with Butlin's for twenty years.

Dancing was so popular with the campers that Bill Butlin decided that the huge dance halls and stages on his camps would be ideal for holding dance festivals. He employed Wilfred Orange who had previously been a chairman of the Official

Board of Ballroom Dancing and had run dance schools and ballrooms before the war to organise them. Wilfred made it possible in 1948 for Butlin's to hold the National Valeta Competition at their Albert Hall Reunion and 5,000 couples took to the dance floor.

The first dance festival was held in 1950 at the Butlin's camp at Pwllheli. It included all types of dancing, from ballet to tap and was so successful that they continue to hold them every year on different camps.

Butlin's for your Holiday, where you make New Friends

After the success and the publicity of the San Carlos Opera Company, Bill Butlin decided that he would give his campers more 'culture'.

The Bristol Old Vic and the International Ballet both performed at the camps and at the opening of the camp at Pwllheli, the Royal Philharmonic Orchestra gave a concert. In the programme there was a solo piano concerto played by Solomon. The work consisted of three movements and during the first one Solomon sat in silence at his piano, with dignified composure.

Bill Butlin and Colonel Basil Brown were standing at the back of the theatre watching the performance, when the resident manager of the camp came up to Bill Butlin and asked him why the pianist wasn't playing? Bill Butlin shrugged his shoulders and replied, 'I suppose Basil hasn't paid him.'

No Matinee unless Wet

In the early 1950s a professional, resident repertory theatre company was started on all the camps and special theatres were built for them. It gave a lot of young campers who came from small, out-of-the-way towns the opportunity to see real actors and actresses for the first time. They put on four to six different performances a week, of such popular plays as, *Rookery*

Bill Butlin with the biggest aspidistra in the world, Gracie Fields.

Nook and *Night Must Fall*. They were all cut down to last for only one hour because Bill Butlin decided that a camper's attention span didn't last any longer.

Performances were always being interrupted by a Redcoat having to get up and turn on the board at the side of the stage which flashed up the 'Crying Baby in Chalet' sign. It always seemed to happen at the most dramatic moment in the play. For example, just as the actor lifted the pillow to suffocate someone, the board would begin to flash frantically, and parents would shuffle out of their seats to go and see to their child.

Before the war Bill Butlin had bought a theatre which had no supporting pillars inside. This meant everyone of the 2000 members of the audience had a perfect view. He bought it cheaply when it was finished with at the World Trade Fair in Glasgow.

One piece at a time the huge metal framework, the theatre seats, the box office and the stage were taken to the camp at Skegness and reassembled. At the outbreak of war the building wasn't complete-

ly rebuilt. This was left for the Navy to do who used it for showing training films and holding ENSA shows. After the war the theatre was used for putting on professional shows for the campers.

It was Colonel Basil Brown's job, as head of entertainment, to organise these shows which were called Resident Revues, and were made up of sketches and Crazy Gang type jokes. In 1946 over lunch at the Café Royal, Basil Brown asked Chesney Allen to take on the job, along with another agent, of finding and booking acts for the Butlin's shows. There wasn't the money to book the really big stars, but Butlin's found that they didn't need names to attract the campers as they would come anyway.

Basil Brown would usually suggest the popular type of acts they needed such as jugglers, magicians, ventriloquists, singers and dancers, and the agent would try and provide them.

Once the show was on, Basil Brown would tour the camps with the agent, seeing how the acts were coping. A lot of the performers who were used to working in smaller theatres found it difficult to

149

The camps are alive to the sound of Julie

adjust to a large audience.

In 1946 Basil Brown gave Richard Stone a newsagent, his first job putting on Resident Revue shows at the Butlin's camps at Skegness, Clacton, Filey and Pwllheli. They staged four different shows over two weeks, with two comedians, a speciality act, a soprano, a soubrette and four chorus girls, provided by Marie De Vere, who came with their own customes and dance routines. They were paid £4 a week plus food and board and they worked for a twenty-week season. There were no understudies.

Richard Stone's instructions from Basil Brown were to find cheap young comedians who had their own props and told clean jokes. He went with Ian Carmichael, who produced the Butlin's shows, and sometimes Basil Brown, to watch possible acts at the Chiswick Empire and the Metropole, Edgware Road.

Two of the first artists he put in for the summer season of 1947 were Terry Scott and Bill Williams, later Bill Maynard. They were working separately. Terry Scott was paid twelve pounds a week, and Bill Maynard eleven pounds. They earned ten shillings extra for doing the company laundry.

David Croft (co-writer of the television series 'Hi De Hi' and 'Dads Army') was a props boy who became the producer.

BARBARA JULIE & TED ANDREWS

Above, accordionist Hetty Brayne.
Left, The Beverly Sisters.
Right, Rock duo Cliff and Sammy.
Above right, Ringo Starr with Rory Storm
and the Hurricanes.

WILFRED ORANGE
AND HIS
ARD GOTHIC (LOUIS XVI) CONCERT HARP.

'A Poached Egg Sat Down on a Piece of Toast'

One night Basil Brown arrived at Pwllheli and stood at the back of the theatre with Richard and watched the show. The comedian was on and after a few minutes Basil Brown turned to Richard and said, 'He's not very good. He'll have to go.' Richard asked when and Basil replied firmly, 'Tonight'.

Richard went back to his chalet in a state of panic. He had to find a replacement as fast as possible. He flicked through a copy of The Stage and saw an advertisement for a comedian called Cliff Weir. He telephoned him to find out if he was available. He was and he said he'd performed in army concert parties during the war, which was fine because the Resident Revue shows at Butlin's were very similar. Richard then telephoned Ian Carmichael and arranged for him to meet Cliff Weir at Paddington Station. If he thought he was funny, and if he had his own props – a revolving bow tie, or a hat with a train running round the brim – Ian was to send him on up to Pwllheli.

The comedian passed the Ian Carmichael test, and arrived at Pwllheli the following day. Basil Brown and Richard stood at the back of the theatre and watched his performance. He sang a song called, 'A Poached Egg Sat Down On A Piece Of Toast'.

Richard realised that although he had performed in army concert parties during the war, it was probably the First World War, not the Second!

Basil Brown turned to Richard Stone and said, 'He's not very good. He'll have to go.' Richard agreed and asked when. Basil replied, 'Tonight'. Richard rushed back to his chalet and again thumbed through his copy of The Stage. He eventually managed to hire Freddie Frinton, who went down very well with the campers and with Basil Brown.

Ian Carmichael directed Butlin's Resident Revue shows from 1947 to 1950. Work was thin on the ground at the time, and he took the Butlin's job although he was only paid £10 a show, because he had a wife and baby to support. He and Richard Stone would meet with Colonel Basil Brown and various camp entertainment managers each February and would be told what was wanted. The shows were just over an hour long, straight through, with no interval. Ian found himself not only directing, but sometimes writing and finding costumes. They rehearsed in drill halls around Swiss Cottage and the costumes were made by a couple of elderly women working in the basement of Barry Bucknell's house. There were no programmes for the shows, they were just known as Resident Revue no. 1 and no. 2 and there were no billings. All the performers were anonymous.

The singer would be accompanied by the camp pianist and there was a small orchestra.

One season they had a woman who played the xylophone. After the first night she complained that she hadn't had time to rehearse with the orchestra, and when Ian Carmichael went to see her in her chalet to assure that everything was all right, he found her sawing bits off her xylophone, accusing it of being out of tune.

By the 1950s the shows had improved. The chorus line had grown from four girls to twelve, and there was a full pit orchestra.

Left, Peter Brough and 'Archie' at Filey 1949.
Right, Tommy Steele with the key to the door, Ayr 1958.
Inset, Tommy Steele with Mike & Bernie Winters.

'Who's the best house?'
'Kent'
'No. Maxwell House'

Bye-Bye Bygraves

Look into my eyes Chuckie

Above, Des O'Connor, and left, always full of fun, Max Bygraves bids fond farewell to Kay Bury at the end of the 1954 season.

'Could the winner of yesterday's bingo move his Rolls Royce because Billy Butlin can't get his bike in.'

Every Night, something Awful!

Peter Casson, the hypnotist, was working for ENSA (Entertainments National Services Association) during the war. In 1946 he got his first professional engagement at the Butlin's camps, for £55 a week. His show lasted an hour and at first he performed in the dining-room after lunch, but the clatter of knives and forks was very distracting, so the show was moved to 11.30 in the evening when it was thought the atmosphere would be more eerie. By then the campers had finished singing 'Penny on the drum', and the children were all safely asleep in their chalets.

Peter kept a couple of bantam hens who scratched around happily outside his chalet and laid eggs, which the chef would cook him for breakfast. But he didn't just keep the chickens for their eggs, they were an important part of his act.

Hypnosis was very new to the general public, and in order to convince them of its powers, Peter would draw his audience's attention at the start of his act by hypnotising a chicken. He would gently lay the chicken on its back, draw an imaginary line in front of its beak and in a matter of seconds its eyes would close, and it would lie motionless, as if it were sleeping. It would remain totally still in that position until Peter clicked his fingers and immediately the chicken would start to cluck and flap its wings around like a normal chicken should.

Then he would ask for volunteers from the audience to come on stage and be hypnotised. Once they were under hypnosis he would make them laugh at comedy and cry at tragedy. To prove that they were unable to feel pain, he would stick a sterile mortician's needle into their arm and draw a spot of blood. At this point it was usual for some members of the audience, generally big, strong-looking men, to faint

Hypnotist
Peter Casson

and the Butlin's Keep Fit Team would have to rush in and carry them out of the theatre. They would be layed out in the foyer, which was nicknamed Casson's Padded Cell, and put behind screens. When they had recovered they always returned to watch the rest of the show.

Peter's hypnosis act was so popular that he travelled from one camp to another. During the day when he wasn't performing he would spend his time wandering round the camp watching the different entertainments. He saw the Amazing Marlow who did a thought-reading act, which consisted of Miss Tree sitting at the piano whilst the Amazing Marlow walked round the theatre getting members of the audience to whisper a tune into his ear. Miss Tree would immediately start to play it without being told what it was.

There was Tiny Evans, the 7ft 9inch giant, who went round the camp signing autographs and saying 'Hello' to the campers, and a one-legged diver called One-Legged Peg, and another one who had only one hand.

One day a diver was standing at the top of an 80 foot ladder ready to jump into the pool, and the Redcoat, who was compering the show, was telling the audience that if the diver made one false move he could crack his skull open. He successfully built up the tension to such a pitch that eventually the diver was so frightened he was unable to make the dive.

Dotted all over the camp were fortune-tellers in booths, which were open late into the night and at the Sunday Night Concerts, Peter watched Izzy Bonn sing, 'My Yiddisher Momma' and 'Let Bygones Be Bygones'.

By the summer season of 1947 Peter Casson had become a household name and Butlin's couldn't afford to employ him. But hypnosis had become such a popular entertainment that Butlin's were able to get hypnotists for only £18 a week, and they put one on every camp site.

Norman Bradford
first Redcoat

When the first camp opened there were plenty of facilities for indoor entertainment, such as billiards and table tennis, darts and dancing. These were all fairly well-used by the new campers, but they hardly touched the outdoor bowling greens and tennis courts.

The campers lack of enthusiasm to join in was something that concerned Bill Butlin. He thought he had provided them with everything, even if the weather was bad, but when he watched them they were just wandering aimlessly around, keeping in tight-knit family groups. They were behaving as they had done on their day trips to the sea side. They weren't used to all the free facilities.

Bill Butlin decided that there had to be some way of getting them out of their shell and mixing with one another. Three days after they opened, he asked Norman Bradford, who started working for him in the 1920s at his amusements at Olympia, if he could think of some way to liven things up. He was a maintenance man during the day and performed a comedy act in the evening. His instructions were to get the campers to mingle. That evening Norman Bradford bounced onto the stage, performed his usual comedy routine and then asked the campers if they would all turn to the person on their right, introduce themselves and shake hands. The campers appeared to be embarrassed, but reluctantly did as they were told. Then they had to do the same with the person on their left. This time they smiled, and giggled, and then they laughed, and shook hands with great friendliness. Suddenly the dining room was buzzing with campers chatting to one another.

The Birth Of The Reds

Bill Butlin was delighted, and congratulated Norman. He told him to go to Skegness the following day and get himself a bright distinctive coloured jacket, so the campers could spot him. Norman Bradford

went to Allan Wildman's clothing shop which supplied 'bum freezer' white jackets for the bar staff, and yellow and blue overalls for the women workers, all with the name 'Butlin's' embroidered on the lapel.

Norman chose three blazers, a blue one, a yellow one, and a white one, and took them back to show Bill Butlin. Although these were the camp colours, Bill Butlin wanted Norman to wear something brighter, something which would make him stand out from everyone else. He decided on a bright red blazer with the letter 'B' on the breast pocket, and white flannels. Allan Wildman made them up, and a week later the first red coat was finished, and Norman Bradford jumped onto the stage at breakfast time wearing it.

He shouted 'Good Morning' to all the campers, and they all shouted back enthusiastically, 'Good Morning'. Then he told them what the day's activities were. The campers laughed and smiled and

Laurel and Hardy working the 1948 season at Skegness, surround

★★★★★★★★★★★★★★★★★★★★★★★★★

obviously enjoyed having someone in charge of their entertainment.

Bill Butlin went back to Allan Wildman's shop and collected more red coats and white flannels. He picked ten friendly young men and women who were working on the camp and told them to put them on. They were the first Redcoats, and it was their job to help the campers to enjoy themselves and join in. They organised card games, draughts, billiards and sports. If it rained they got the band out regardless of the time of day, and held a dance. They made sure there was always something to do, a regatta on the boating lake, or swimming competitions in the pool. The Redcoats organised midnight hikes. Six or seven hundred campers would follow Norman Bradford out of the camp and along the beach, where they'd light a huge bonfire. A couple of musicians from the dance band would bring out an accordion and a saxophone, and there would follow a sing-song, which went on for an hour or

y Redcoats

more, until the tired campers sang their way back to their chalets at about three in the morning.

Butlin's Showtime

In the evening the dining room doubled as a theatre. After dinner, the campers picked up their chairs and lined them up in rows in front of the small stage, ready for a show.

Those early shows were pretty amateur as Bill Butlin could not afford to employ expensive professional performers. There was a local five-piece band and a mouth organist called Jimmy Flaherty. Jimmy Loft, a local pub owner, and Frank Cusworth, who had worked on the Dodgems during the summer, performed a contortionist dancing act, and Norman Bradford told some stand-up gags. Sometimes Bill Butlin overcame his shyness, and helped Norman Bradford out with his act.

Bill Butlin would walk onto the stage looking very sad, and Norman would ask him why he was so miserable. Bill Butlin would explain that it was because Georgie the elephant had just died. 'I didn't know you liked elephants,' Norman Bradford would reply. 'I don't,' said Bill Butlin, 'but I've got to bury him'.

Campers were encouraged to go onto the stage and perform, in order to pad out the show. They usually sang 'Come Into The Garden, Maud', which was the most popular song of the day, and they usually sang it dreadfully out of tune. The shows weren't good – they were terrible – and Bill Butlin realised that he had to find a way of improving them. He went to a friend, Bert Aza, who was a show business agent, and asked him what his artists did on a Sunday. He was told they either travelled or rested. Bill Butlin asked if they could perform at his camp on a Sunday. He'd pay them the usual fee, which as they weren't normally working was an added bonus to their earnings.

A few week later Butlin's put on

A REDCOAT is also **an individual, a character, a personality girl (or boy), a sporting type, a sing-song leader, a bingo caller, a children's uncle, a swimmer, a dancer,** but – above all – **a mixer, a mingler.**

their first Sunday concert. It starred Norman Evans, the famous female impersonator, who was paid twelve pounds ten shillings for performing his monologue, 'Over The Garden Wall'. The big name stars were a great attraction, as most of the campers couldn't afford to go and se live shows, but the ones at Butlin's were free. Over the next few months the stars of the day arrived at Butlin's. There were Elsie and Doris Waters, Florence Desmond, Will Fyfe, Ted Ray, Albert Wheelan and Harry Champion who sang 'Any Old Iron'.

Over the next couple of years the camp had a regular stream of celebrities. The most famous was Gracie Fields, who was topping the bill at the London Palladium at the time for £1,200 a week. Amy Johnson, who had just set a new record for a solo flight from England to Australia paid a visit, and Len Hutton arrived the day after he'd scored 364 runs at the Oval.

A year later the five-piece band was replaced by Mantovani and his orchestra and Lew Stone and his band. Victor Sylvester gave ballroom dancing lessons and Len Harvey, the British light heavyweight champion, gave boxing lessons, and not always to the campers. At one session he used a kangaroo as a sparring partner. Dan Maskell coached the campers in tennis, and Victor Barnes in table tennis. Joe Davis and Horace Lindrum played snooker.

'Hi-De-Hi', 'Ho-De-Ho'

Half way through the first summer season, there was a popular American film doing the rounds at the cinemas. In it there was a scene where someone shouted out 'Hi-De-Hi' and a crowd of people called back 'Ho-De-Ho'. That film was probably Cab Calloway's 'Hi-De-Hi', and it was very popular. Norman Bradford, the original Redcoat, just like everyone else, had been to see the film. He was so taken by the 'Hi-De-Hi' catch phrase, that one morning when he jumped onto the stage to say

hello to the campers, he called out 'Hi-De-Hi' to them. To his surprise all the campers replied with the shout, 'Ho-De-Ho'. From then on whenever a Redcoat wanted everyone's attention in order to make an announcement, they began by calling out 'Hi-De-Hi', the campers would reply with a 'Ho-De-Ho', and then the announcement was given. The expression caught on so fast that when ever a camper was walking along and bumped into a Redcoat, the words 'Hi-De-Hi', 'Ho-De-Ho' would pass between them.

Cheetah Races

In 1939 Geraint James was a 17-year-old student at Cambridge University. During his summer vacation he worked as a Redcoat at Butlin's. When he arrived there were about 4,000 campers, all behaving very informally. Along with the other new Redcoats he was greeted with a 'Hi-De-Hi' from Norman Bradford, which seemed very strange, but after a while he found he was saying 'Hi-De-Hi' to campers, a thousand times a day.

For working as a Redcoat he was given free food and board, and after a month he was paid a £1 a week. His job was a Redcoat sports organiser, and the first thing he was given to do was hand out the roller skates. Later he organised the tennis, golf and swimming, and drove a little brightly coloured vehicle like a milk float, which went around the site so that campers could hop on and off for a ride. In the evening he had to either sit or dance with the campers. The rule was that a Redcoat must never spend the evening with one female camper, and certainly not just pick out the prettiest to dance with.

At the far end of the camp there was a stadium where pig, cheetah and greyhound racing was held. Geraint James was given the job of catching them after the race with a dog collar and a piece of rope. At first he was very scared of the cheetahs, but he soon found that they were tame, quiet harmless and easy to catch. He had to put them in the animal quarters, where campers could leave their pets whilst they were on holiday.

Godfrey Winn, Kay, Countess Mountbatten, Bill Butlin, Archbishop of York.

'Countess Mountbatten came to the camp for three days and loved it!'

Kay Bury went to Butlin's, with her husband, as a camper in 1936. She enjoyed every minute of it, and wanted to be a Redcoat, but her husband wouldn't let her. During the war they were divorced, and Kay returned to Butlin's camp at Filey in 1945, this time not as a camper but as a Redcoat.

'It was 1945 and the camp at Filey was half full of holiday makers and still half full of troops. I was the manager's secretary, hostess and Redcoat, then I did everything. In the twenty years I was a Chief Redcoat Hostess at Butlin's I worked at all the camps, later I trained new Redcoats.

One of my early jobs was to look after the artists who came down for the Sunday concert party shows. The telex would tell us that someone like Terry Thomas,

Charlie Chester or Anona Wynn was arriving and I'd arrange for them to have a nice chalet and for a car to collect them from the station. When they arrived on the camp, I'd take them to the theatre so they could do a run through of their act. We had two theatres on most camps and I'd make sure they got from one to the other in time for the next show.

In 1949 we had the Young Conservative Rally at Filey Camp. My job was to look after Anthony Eden. That same year we had the Young Labour Party Conference at the same camp, and Herbert Morrison visited several times.

Later on in the season, Countess Mountbatten also came to Filey, and bought her daughter Pamela for three days, they both loved it.

I loved singing in the Pig & Whistle Bar, sometimes to 3,000 campers, and I'd get them all singing popular songs of the day: 'Nellie Dean', 'Hokey Cokey', 'Boomps-A-Daisy', 'The Palais Glide'. In 1948 there was a BBC broadcast from Filey camp, and I led the sing-song. I was the first person at Butlin's to play skiffle, 'Rock Island Line,' and 'Bring A Little Water Sylvie'.

Around 1951 I was sent to Nassau, where Bill Butlin had opened a hotel and I worked there for a while. It was around the time that the Queen, then Princess Elizabeth, did square dancing whilst she was in Canada, and it got a lot of publicity. Bill Butlin decided that he'd have his own Butlin's square dancing team on the camps, so another Redcoat and I were told to go to New York and learn to square dance. When we returned to England I had to go round all the camps and teach a team of Redcoats, all in full western costume, square dancing. The Butlin's square dancing team became very famous on the camps, and in the winter we travelled to functions at The Savoy, The Ritz and The Grosvenor House Hotel doing square dancing as the cabaret spot. We'd do it and

A REDCOAT works a hard and tiring day –
whose ready smile is just as genuine last thing at
night as it was at breakfast-time.

then we'd get the audience up to join in.

At Clacton camp I had my own bar, called Kay's Bar, and I'd have literally thousands of campers in there all singing away. Ted and Barbara Andrews came to do Sunday night concerts on the camp circuit, and one night their daughter Julie, who was only thirteen at the time, stood at the door of my bar and asked if she could come in and sing. Although she was under age, she brought the house down.

In the winter I was Chief Hostess at the Butlin's hotels, as well as having a desk at the head office in Oxford Street. When the Butlin's camp opened at Bognor I was given the job of going round the area knocking on people's doors, asking them if they had spare bedrooms for the season, to rent to Butlin's staff. In the first year 500 Butlin's employees at Bognor were living outside of the camp, because there wasn't enough room on the site. I hated the job of organising digs for them. Once they'd taken my red coat away, I didn't want to be there anymore. After twenty years as a Butlin's Redcoat, and Chief Hostess, I left.**'**

'I didn't realise you were the boss's son'

In 1950 when Bobby Butlin was 16 he was a Redcoat one summer during his school holidays.

'I hadn't got anything planned for my school holiday, so my Father sent me to his camp at Ayr in Scotland, to be a Redcoat. I had to live on the camp, just like all the other Reds, and I was paid £7. I knew the system because I'd been round the camps all my life. I arrived on a Saturday and I was stuck into a red coat straight away, feeling awful. I'm not a sort of hail-fellow-well-met sort of person, and I didn't really like having to be pleasant to everybody all the time. I didn't really get off to a good start, because on my first night I was caught in a girl camper's chalet, and the next morning I was hauled up in

front of the general manager who gave me a real ticking off, being the boss's son and everything I think he was told to treat me a bit more severely than everybody else. The irony of it was the girl and her parents left a couple of days later and I received a letter from the mother (she was the one who had caught me) saying that she hadn't realised who I was when she'd thrown me out of her daughter's chalet, and she was very sorry and next time I was passing through Warrington, I was free to call in.**'**

Paddy Hope first worked for Butlin's in 1952, a year later she became a Redcoat at Ayr, Clacton, Filey and Pwllheli.

'When I was 20 I went to work as a secretary at the Heads of Ayr, the Butlin's Hotel. In the evening I was a Redcoat in the ballroom, and like the other Redcoats in Scotland I had to wear a kilt. Bobby Butlin was a Redcoat at Ayr for that season, and all of us girls were all told not to spoil him because he was the boss's son, we weren't supposed to do any washing for him, or iron his shirts. We just had to treat him like one of the lads. I don't think he particularly enjoyed it. He was very shy, but he tried. At the beginning of every week we had to go onto the stage and be introduced to the new campers, Bobby would often go on in his kilt and tip up his sporran when he was introduced, which caused quite a giggle amongst the girls.

A year later I went to Clacton Camp, as a Redcoat sports organiser. I was supplied with two Redcoats, a thick one for the day and a thin gaberdene one for the evening, and a white pleated skirt. I had to get my own blouse, shoes, and shorts, the shorts had to show just below the Redcoat. I had always had more more than one of everything to allow for being thrown in the swimming pool.

On a Saturday when the new campers arrived, us girls used to stand in reception to direct them. Really we'd be eyeing up the boys, lining them up for our day off, usually the ones who arrived in nice little sports cars. And on the following Saturday when they left, there would be fond farewells, and we'd see who else was arriving for the next week. **'**

'Des O'Connor hid in the girls' coach'.

Des O'Connor was a Butlin's Redcoat at the camp at Filey in the early fifties. Kay Bury was the Chief Redcoat Hostess at the time and remembers his antics.

'Des was very comical. He was a good Redcoat, he joined in everything. But there are two events that I particularly remember about him. There was one time when it was the last week of the season at Filey, Bill Butlin was on the camp, and Des O'Connor was on the sports field, telling jokes. Now everything a Redcoat said into the microphone could be heard round the camp on the tannoy system. Des told a joke about someone picking their nose, and Bill Butlin, who was in his chalet at the time, heard it. He thought it was very tasteless and sent for Des and told him that

if it hadn't been the last week of the season he would have fired him.

I also remember when I was chaperoning the Butlin's Holiday Princess competitiors at the Albert Hall reunion one year. There was a rule that no male Redcoats were allowed on the coach with the girls. One day I got them all into their coach, and who was hiding on it? Des. He was naughty, I had to throw him off, but it was all in good fun. **'**

'A fat lady and a thin lady were smoking a cigarette. Who finished first?'
'I dunno'
'The fat one. Because she's got bigger drawers'

Ted Rogers was a Redcoat at the Butlin's Ocean Hotel at Brighton in 1959

'An agent suggested I should go and work at Butlin's. So I did. I worked at the Butlin's Ocean Hotel for twenty weeks, for £9 a week, free food and lodgings, and I thought that was great.

Believe it or not I was very shy in those days, and one of the first jobs I was given was standing in reception on a Saturday meeting all the new campers as they arrived. I used to blush and say, 'Hello, how are you? Where are you from?' to everybody. Then I'd have to take thirty or so campers on a ramble, and they'd all want to be talked to, and I didn't know what to say. It was the same with the bingo. I'd think 'God I've got to call the bingo for two hours, how can I make it entertaining', and I'd call out corny things like 'Two little ducks' and the campers would shout back 'Quack Quack'. Then I

had to do the tea dances in the afternoon, and I can't dance, no one had asked me if I could. And of course there was always some old lady who would pick me out, and our feet would be treading on each other's, and I'd have to shuffle round the dance floor.

After five weeks, I was allowed to be in the Redcoat show. It was only a small 600-seater theatre at the hotel. I'd been watching some of the other comedians and they came out with all this old material and brought the house down. Although I'd only been in the business a short time I thought, how can they laugh at this rubbish? Just wait till I get up on that stage. And when I did I told the most terrible gags, and got huge laughs. First of all I was sent on as the warm-up act, but later I was moved to the best spot at the close of the show. Bill Butlin came down on the last

week of the season, and he saw my act, and was quite impressed, so he sent me to the camp at Filey, where the season went on longer than at the hotels. I didn't go as a Redcoat but as part of the revue company. I got there – and saw the size of the theatre, it went on for miles. It was a 3,000-seater. I was terrified. I'd been working with a small audience in a ballroom with a little stage, and suddenly there I was with lights, and this terrible orchestra pit full of musicians, and a front row miles away. I found it very hard to get my act across. I was used to getting laughs on little eye movements, which work on a small audience, but they're lost on a big one. I got out in front of that audience, and I roasted.

You weren't allowed to tell any blue gags, or even use the expression, 'Shut your gob'. You weren't allowed to make jokes about the food. And you weren't allowed to make jokes about the camp being like a big prison. The campers knew I'd made a fool of myself, so it was OK for them too. We also ran a competition called, The Crazy Court, which was a real ad lib show. Two married campers would get up on the stage and pretend they were in court getting divorced. There was a prosecution Redcoat and I played the policeman looking after the husband. The wife always used to give her husband a real grilling, and he'd start getting a red neck and looking really embarrassed. Then the Redcoat prosecution would ask him how he could stand for this, and I'd give him a chair, which always got a laugh.

I only worked one season as a Redcoat, but in 1974 I did the cabaret at the London Palladium where Butlin's were holding the finals of their talent competition. From 1974 to 1981 I worked 9 seasons, 44 one-nighters at various Butlin's camps. I was on the late night cabaret circuit. As well as me there was Vince Hill, Ken Dodd, Bernard Manning and Bob Monkhouse. No children were allowed into these shows, so you could be a bit risqué, and the campers paid extra to get in and sit at separate tables and have a meal. The cabaret started at midnight, and it felt really strange, because a Redcoat used to do the warm-up for me, just like I used to do the warm up for the comedian Jimmy Wheeler

Being a Redcoat at Butlin's was just like working on the QE2, only they wear a different uniform and guests have paid more. **'**

'The campers thought Cliff's music was a racket'

Stan Edwards remembers when Cliff Richard and his group, the Drifters, were bar entertainers at Clacton camp in 1958

'Cliff Richard and the Drifters started off in the Pig and Whistle Bar, where campers used to go for a knees up and a sing song. They thought Cliff's music was a racket and nobody went in there when he was playing. Cliff only knew about eight numbers at the time, and they were all Elvis Presley songs. He used to look like Elvis, and wiggle in the same way. You can imagine the sort of campers who wanted a sing song liking that sort of music! Of course they'd put Cliff in the wrong bar, once they moved him to the South Seas Coffee Bar he went down well, and he did

sessions in the Rock'n'Roll Ballroom, in the afternoon when there was only about thirty people in there. Cliff left after a few weeks. **'**

'Welcome to you
How do you do
Happiness and gaiety are coming
to you
Oceans of fun
For everyone
Everything to make you happy
under the sun
Welcome to Butlin's
Butlin's by the sea'

'Hello My Darlings'
Charlie Drake worked as a Redcoat at Butlin's Filey camp in 1957. He was out of work at the time and couldn't get a summer season. His agent suggested he audition for Butlin's.

'I went to Butlin's head office in Oxford Street and did my fifteen minute comedy act. When I came off the stage they said they heard I did Ju Jitsu, would I like to teach it on the camp? That's what they thought of my comedy act. I was so broke that I took the job. The money wasn't good but the food, clothes and accommodation were free. I took my wife and baby, and we were given our own little chalet, which we made very homely. My wife got a job as a Radio Butlin girl, doing the broadcasts. I thought the camp was huge. There were middle class and working class people there, and they all mixed in.

As a Redcoat my first job was to teach the female Redcoats Ju Jitsu, which is self-defence, which they could use against the more amorous campers. But then I had to teach it to the campers so that they could defend themselves against the more amorous Redcoats. I also did wrestling and boxing matches, and because I'm a little bloke, these great vast men used to come up to me and say, 'Who's going to teach us

A REDCOAT is a 'team-worker' – a member of a Happy Gang whose aim is to ensure that Butlin holiday-makers have the greatest vacation of their lives.

to look after ourselves then?' I had some pretty hairy times. I felt it couldn't go on, so one day I broke a camper's shoulder. I did it on purpose to put a stop to it, before I got hurt, and it worked. Bill Butlin ordered no more Ju Jitsu on the camp.

I used to give a talk in the boxing ring, and call up campers to help with some demonstration wrestling. I wanted to do this hold which is called 'the laughing

death' where I put both hands, in a certain position on someone's shoulders, whilst talking and smiling at them, and they go into a comatose state. Then I bring them out of it. I told the entertainments man that I'd like to do this. He said OK, but not on a camper, in case I couldn't get them out of it. The camp vicar, Will Curtis, volunteered to be the victim. He'd come into the ring, wearing his dog collar, and I'd say I was sending him to heaven, and out he'd go like a light, and then I'd bring him back. The campers loved it.

Our job was to make sure campers had a good time, all the time. We had to dance with them in the ballrooms, and we weren't allowed to stay with one girl, we had to put ourselves about. Women campers would really dress up, they'd bring whole wardrobes of clothes, and men would wear suits. Ballroom dancing

was very popular.

We had to sit with the campers at meal times and help them plan their day. We took them on nature walks and pony treks and every week there was a sports day and an aqua show, when I did some comedy diving. For the older campers there were handicraft exhibitions and lectures, whist drives and old time dancing.

Us Redcoats were aunts and uncles for the day, and we had to work in a sort of 'kiddies' corral', where there were slides, rides and sweets for the children. Parents would lose their kids on purpose. We'd find them crying, and take them into the corral and fuss them, and they could stay there until their parents were found. But we'd see the parents peeping over the fence, checking their child was safe, and then they'd go off and have a nice quiet day away from them.

One of my other duties was calling out the tombola numbers, it's what we call bingo now, and that's how I supplemented my income. I cheated. I sold the tickets and worked out a system where, although I doubled the takings, I was making £60 a week, cash. No one at Butlin's knew how I was doing it, even though they had the security men in to watch me. I did it for a whole season and at the end of it Bill Butlin came and had a drink with the Redcoats. He asked me back the following year, but I told him the wages weren't good enough, and he said, 'Well, if you tell me how you've been robbing me of £60 every week in the bingo, I'll double your wages'. He knew what was going on, but I didn't tell him, and I decided to go back the following season.

During the evening I did six shows a week in the theatre, some stand up comedy, old time musicals and reviews. At the side of the stage there was a big board with a flashing light on it, and just as you'd be in the middle of a joke, you'd hear beep-beep and 'A baby crying in chalet number 58, or somewhere' would flash up on the board. It always happened right in the middle of the joke and ruined the act. No blue gags were allowed, not even by the visiting artists, and no swearing, not even the word 'bloody'. The quiz show 'What's My Line?' was a favourite amongst the campers. The Redcoats would be the celebrities and the campers would be the contestants. I still get letters from campers who remember me when I was a Redcoat.

They were great days. **"**

Stan on floor, Don Cook middle, and Roy Hudd mudlarking at the Clacton regatta 1958

'Are you musicians?'
'Yes'
'Right. Move that piano.'

In 1958 an agent saw Roy Hudd performing his double act, and offered him and his partner a job at Butlin's. They signed the contract thinking they'd just got themselves work as entertainers. When they arrived at the camp at Clacton, they were very surprised to be handed red coats.

'When I arrived at Clacton camp the season hadn't started. After realising that I wasn't there just an entertainer but as a Redcoat, I was thrown straight in the deep end; moving pianos, marking out the football pitches, crawling on ladders across the indoor swimming pool to hang up hundreds of plastic sea-gulls.

When the new campers arrived on a Saturday, there'd be these stunning-looking Redcoats in reception. The blokes used to love this. But they weren't really Redcoats, they were dancers in the review company. All they ever did as Redcoat duties was welcome the campers on a Saturday. They were like window dressing. The poor geezers who had seen these fantastic looking birds, when they arrived, used to spend the rest of the week trying to find them again. Of course they never did.

I had to referee football matches, which was hysterical when you had 22 campers who didn't know the rules, and neither did I. The number of matches I refereed that were abandoned half way through, and I was chased the other end of the camp because I'd given a wrong decision. I had to teach roller skating, and I couldn't skate, so I used to shout out instructions from the side. If it rained we had 'Games if wet', which we put on in the Viennese ballroom.

The campers really took their inter-house competitions very seriously, it was like being back at school. I remember one pram race when I was pushing this old girl in a pram, she was about eighty, and I was galloping along at a great rate and she was shouting at me, 'Come on, love, get to the front, we've got to win for York House'. Suddenly we hit a stone or something in the path, and the pram tipped over and she shot out and hit her head on the concrete. She was out cold, unconscious, and I thought, 'Blimey I've killed a camper'. I went with her to the medical centre, and sat with her. When she started to come round the first thing she said was, 'Did we win?' That's how keen people were.

We started work at 7.00 in the morning, entertaining the campers at breakfast. I only weighed eight stone then and the camp comic used to pick me up and hang me on a coat hook just inside the dining hall, it got a great laugh, but I hated it that early. You worked right on through six days a week, until midnight, when I did the midnight cabaret.

On our day off my pal and I were so whacked we used to sleep till three in the afternoon. We had an identity card and on the back of it is used to say something about how these people had saved for 50 weeks of the year, and it was our job to make sure that they had the greatest fortnight of their lives. It was a real brainwashing job. I got to the stage where I really believed this, and I'd stagger out of bed and read the back of my identity card and think, 'They're right, I will give them a good time'. Well, after 24 weeks of this sort of work pressure I just blew my stack, and the medical officer put me in a darkened room for three days, just to get myself together again. On the fourth day I came out beaming and bouncing again.

I remember Bill Butlin visiting the camp. It was like God coming, we all had to be on our toes and lined up in the dining hall. He walked through with his entourage behind him, saying 'Hi' to us. When he got to the end of this 2,000-seater hall, he stood at the door and said to one of his aides, 'There's a sauce bottle with a torn label on table 17'. We all thought it was terrific.

One night there was a terrible thunder storm and the top end of the camp was flooded. It was where the new sophisticated South Seas Coffee Bar had just opened. It had glass tables with live gold fish, and was really sprauncey. The place was three feet deep in water, and the drains couldn't take any more. We were all woken up at three in the morning, and told to get up there and rescue the South Seas Coffee Bar. We were walking up there, and I lost my pal for a while, he disappeared down a drain, but eventually we got to the South Seas Coffee Bar and about 2,000 campers were there, bailing out of the water, cleaning the tables, checking everything was OK as if they were employed by Butlin's. One of them wading

in the water, turned to me and said 'Marvellous isn't it?, just like the blitz.' There was a war-time spirit about Butlin's then, everybody wanted to be together.

The old campers who had been going since the place started, were the ones to look out for. If you didn't say 'Good morning' to them, or smile, they'd report you. You had to smile eighteen hours a day. It got to the stage with the smiling that when my pal and I left Butlin's after six months, at the end of the season, we walked up Oxford Street smiling at everybody. People turned round and stared at us. They wondered what was wrong with these blokes, because nobody walks round London, smiling. **?**

Butlin's security man on chalet patrol: 'Have you got a girl in there?'
'No'
'Then I'll throw one in'

Freddie 'Parrot Face' Davies was working as an undertaker for the Co-op when he got a job as a Butlin's Redcoat in 1958

'I went to Butlin's and was interviewed by six entertainment managers. I told them I wanted to be a Redcoat because I wanted to get into show business. I said, 'Yes' to everything I couldn't do on the application form, and I got the job. Free food and board and £6 10s a week.

I arrived at Skegness camp to start when and it wasn't due to open for a week. There were about thirty of us Redcoats and we had to paint the rostrums for the Holiday Princess competition, and get out the roller skates and tart them up. I was given a Redcoat, two nylon shirts and five badges of the different camps which had to be worn in a certain order. We were told we had to smile and be friendly at all times. We weren't allowed to swear or enter a camper's chalet and we couldn't drink, except a shandy, whilst on duty. We were given a book of vouchers worth seven shillings so we could buy ourselves coffee in the coffee bar whilst sitting with the campers. Early on in 1961 I was made Assistant Entertainment Manager, and gave up my red coat for a blue blazer, and I was given a bicycle to ride around the camp on, but it kept on getting stolen.

By 1963 I was made Deputy Entertainment Manager at the camp at Minehead,

and I compèred all the competitions. My son was christened in the church on the camp during the lunch hour, when the amusements stopped. But I'd got a wife and children by then and I was only earning fourteen pounds ten shillings a week, and I couldn't afford to live on Butlin's pay, so I wrote to an agent, and left. **'**

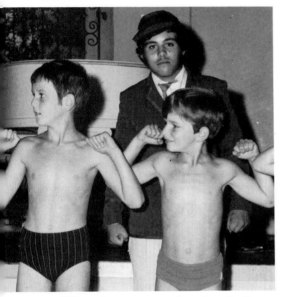

'What do you mean there's a fire? Do your tie up'.

Andy Ayliffe went to Butlin's with his parents, in 1963, when he was ten years old. In the 'Tarzan' competition, he had to parade around in his bathing costume, showing off his bare chest. He won a cup and a voucher worth ten shillings. His family won the Happy Family competition, and got a free holiday the following season. Andy decided then that he wanted to be a Redcoat. He thought they were the nearest thing he'd ever met to a comic-book hero.

'We weren't given any training, just told to smile a lot. We weren't ever allowed to say 'I don't know', it had to be, 'I'll find out'. I enjoyed running all the competitions. We had some funny ones, like the Number 6 cigarette competition. We'd ask all the campers who smoked Number 6, and there would be a big show of hands, because they were very popular in those days. Then we'd ask them to each put one cigarette in a box, and then they had to identify their cigarette. Of course they couldn't, so we ended up with about 300 free cigarettes. Then there were the team races. On a Sunday morning, we had a hunt-the-parrot competition, whoever found him, won the £5 note in his beak. Of course there wasn't a parrot and there wasn't a £5 note. Then we got half a dozen raw eggs and told the campers they were hard boiled and the competition was to throw them at each other, getting further apart. Egg was everywhere.

One night we heard the fire alarms and went to look, and the Blinking Owl Bar was burning. I started helping to evacuate people and to get the fire extinguishers. There was a crowd of campers standing around watching. I undid my bow tie, and was overcome with the fumes and went off to get a cup of coffee. I bumped into the manager, who told me to do my bow tie up! I worked one Christmas holiday. Some of the campers were self-catering, but everyone got a present from Father Christmas and there was a full Christmas dinner and a tot of rum with breakfast. Miss Holiday Princess was renamed Miss Mistletoe. **'**

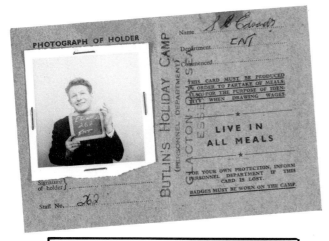

1 Redcoats. Centre: entertainments manager.

Staff pass. Reverse side, 'Your duty to the camper holidaymaker civility, courtesy and service with a smile at all times. You work in a holiday atmosphere to provide rest and happiness for many hundred of your fellow beings every week. They depend on your efforts for a brief respite from their everyday labours, and it is part of their holiday to be waited upon, to find comfort, relaxation and entertainment.' The Butlin's motto, 'The Camper is always right'.

Dave Allen was unable to get a job on a newspaper when he arrived in England in 1955 so he became a Butlin's Redcoat. He used to ride bikes off the top of the diving board and have soda syphon battles in the

5 From left to right: waitress, chef, waiter, supervisor.

6 Left: Chalet maids. Right: supervisors.

2 Old green musician's jacket.   3 Left: supervisor. Right: bar staff.   4 Nursery nurses. Centre: old uniform.

bar. Cliff Richard was a bar entertainer. Russ Hamilton who became a fifties pop star, was a 'Kiddies' Uncle'.

Behind the scenes, Glenda Jackson was a waitress in the coffee bar at the camp at Filey. At Ayr, the actor Bill Simpson was working in the cashier's office and Scottish singer Moira Anderson worked in the accommodation department.

Hi-de-Ho!

7 Tracksuits and sports wear for Redcoats.

8 New security uniform.

169

9 Old security cap, jacket and armband.

'Sweet 16 never been kissed
Sweet 16 never been to Butlin's
If you haven't been to Butlin's
You haven't lived.'

BUTLIN'S

Wall to Wall Crumpet

The 'Swinging Sixties' brought a new breed of holiday maker, single teenagers. They had money and the freedom to go on holiday without their parents. They leapt onto their Lambrettas and into their Ford Cortinas and they headed for Butlin's, where there was free entertainment during the evening and free activities during the day. Unlike a hotel there was very little security. People could come and go when ever they wanted. At home there was just the pub and a dance on a Saturday night. At Butlin's there were rock 'n' roll ballrooms, juke boxes, coffee bars and special teenage chalets. These could sleep four in double bunk beds with a ten shilling reduction for sharing. During the summer months it wasn't unusual to find 3,000 single young people at one camp in any one week.

To keep them separate from families who wanted to be quiet, teenagers were given their own section of the dining room but it didn't stop them from throwing food at one another. And later on, they were given their own chalet lines, at the far end of each site with the boys in one row and the girls in another, which were patrolled by security men. It didn't prevent the all night chalet parties that went on until dawn, when half-dressed teenagers could be seen clutching bundles of clothing, tip-toeing across the grass back to their chalets.

Tony Peers was 16 when he went to Butlin's at Pwllheli. 'Butlin's was the place to go' he recalls, 'it was utopia for us teenagers. There were thousands of us and we all walked around without our parents for the first time, and we felt really grown up. Butlin's was glamorous. There were live bands and the place was crawling with girls. We sat in the coffee bar during the day playing the juke box and chatting up the crumpet. At night we packed into the rock 'n' roll ballroom. It was a struggle to get to the bar and we got brainless every

Below,
Jackie
Styler

night. There were security patrols and they'd come round and throw the girls out of your chalet, 'cos they weren't supposed to be there. The wonderful thing about Butlin's was that for the first time for all of us, there was booze, girls and somewhere to take them.'

170

Bob Chalk, first on right

Winkle Pickers at Butlin's

Bob Chalk was 17 when he went to Butlin's at Skegness in 1961. For him, and the 20 friends that he went with, it was their first holiday without their parents. When they arrived they found that the camp was full of single young teenagers.

During the day they played football and hung around the coffee bar and in the evening they packed into the dance hall. The girls wore fashionable short dresses with full skirts which had layers of stiff petticoats underneath. Bob and his friend were thrown out of the ballroom for putting a mirror on the floor, just outside the ladies room, so that when the girls stepped over it the boys could see up their skirts. The final straw was when one of them rode their motor bike through the ballroom.

If it was hot at night the teenagers would drag their mattresses out of their chalets and onto the grass.

Towards the middle of the 1960s the gang fights started and the teenagers began to vandalise the camps. One night the security men evicted a hundred of them from one camp site. Butlin's was beginning to get bad publicity and, according to Bobby Butlin, a reputation for being 'a glorified knocking shop without money changing hands'. Families who had always been to Butlin's were being driven away. Finally in 1968 Butlin's stopped group bookings from single teenagers.

The Butlin's Times are A-Changing

In 1965 the expansion and building programmes which had seen some Butlin's sites grow so large they could now accommodate 11,000 people, were stopped. For the first time Butlin's had started to lose business.

Bill Butlin retired in 1968 and went to live in Jersey, leaving his son Bobby to run the company. It was suffering from bad publicity and competition from overseas package holidays.

The late 1960s were bad years. The holiday makers who had stayed faithful to them for four decades had started to change their lifestyle and their habits, and Butlin's hadn't kept pace with them.

In the 1960s Butlin's were still serving the same menu as ten years previously. Much of the accommodation was still the same chicken wire and cement-walled little chalets. Only now, despite the many coats of brightly coloured paint, they were beginning to look weather beaten and worn. The communal fun and games and the rip roaring hi-jinks of the jovial Redcoats that had been so popular with three previous generations were now shunned by the present one.

One of the first things that Bobby Butlin did when he took over the ailing company, apart from stopping teenage bookings, was to build private bathrooms and self-catering chalets, and convert a large number of existing ones by equipping them with cookers and fridges. This meant that campers had the freedom to either choose to eat in the Butlin's dining hall, or prepare their own.

The word 'dinner' was taken off the

171

Rank takes over

menu and changed to 'evening meal' because a lot of campers had what they called 'dinner' at midday. Butlin's stopped serving lunch and now only provided breakfast in the morning and a meal in the evening. Food venues opened up all over the camp sites providing alternative meals at any time of the day. This, combined with self-catering, meant that the huge number of campers that the kitchens had previously had to cater for was reduced. Now they were able to concentrate on quality rather than quantity.

The bands and the shows, which were Butlin's strong point, remained as star-studded as ever. A midnight cabaret was introduced which excluded children but offered adult campers the change to enjoy night club entertainment. During the day the entertainment for children continued, and in the evening they were safely watched over by the 'night owl' chalet patrols.

By 1971 Butlin's was back on top, with record bookings.

To Lose the Blues Just Spread the News – a Holiday at Butlin's

In 1972 Butlin's was taken over by the Rank Organisation and bigger winds of change began to blow through the camp sites. In 1977 the morning 'Wakey Wakey' call over the Tannoy, reminding campers that they had half an hour to get ready for breakfast, was scrapped. Bobby Butlin

broke the last recording himself.

The old faithful competitions that are still popular with so many campers, Fancy Dress, Knobbly Knees and Glamorous Grandmothers remain.

The churches on each site are still there with a resident padre but the congregations are small these days and although the chaplain is always available, holiday makers don't go to him with their problems the way they used to.

The Redcoats remained, bright and breezy, with a willing smile and a helpful hand but there are now only about thirty on each site and they give more directions and information than tell jokes. They still wear the same smart bright red blazers and run the donkey derby and other weekly competitions. In the ballrooms and the bars they are still persuading women to lift their skirts just that little bit higher to allow everyone to see their lovely legs.

To escape the jokes about prisoner-of-war camps and Colditz, Butlin's decided that the sites were no longer to be called camps, but holiday centres, villages or parks instead, and the campers were to be referred to as 'guests'.

In 1979, Butlin's took over the El Griego hotel in Spain, which has Spanish Red-coats, with names like Manuel, who organise bingo and fancy dress.

Rain Never Stopped Play at Butlin's

In 1980 Butlin's had a peak year with 1.2 million 'guests', so it was something of a shock when three years later the camps at Filey, Clacton and Mosney were closed, leaving Bognor, Minehead, Barry, Skegness, Ayr and Pwllheli.

After selling off three of the sites Rank set about upgrading the accommodation at the other six. New Georgian-style chalets are being built with bow windows. They have names like Sussex and Somerset suites and the chalet lines are called Arundel Way, and have cobbled paths and olde worlde replica lamp posts. Inside

Above, fifty years on – still dodging! Below, saving souls at Butlin's, exterior & interior of new Sussex suite, Bognor

Bye Hi-de-Hi, hello Somerwest!

there is wall-to-wall carpeting, a teasmade, a colour television, fan heater and private bathroom with shower.

Guests who stay in one of these spanking new chalets have their meals in a separate dining room with reserved tables, waitress service and wine as an optional extra with the evening meal. But this is still Butlin's and favourite habits die hard. A pot of tea is still served with the soup and traditional roast chicken is still the favourite meal.

Everything's Big at Butlin's

A Butlin's holiday is still essentially a family one, Mum, Dad and the children. Three years ago one family with sixty relatives took over a whole row of chalets at Skegness. And Butlin's now caters for a type of family that wasn't even talked about in 1936, – single parent families.

They now offer fun pools, helicopter rides and in the spring, children's Venture Weeks.

Once a year the Salvation Army and the Seventh Day Adventists hold a religious week at Bognor, and the bars, bingo and slot machines are closed down.

There are international ballroom dancing championships, darts tournaments, jazz festivals and brass band contests.

In the autumn of 1985 Butlin's announced that they were spending £9 million on revamping the centre at Minehead. It is to be relaunched in the summer of 1986 under the name Somerwest World, with de-luxe accommodation. It will have an enclosed water playground called the Sunsplash Club, with three sixty-foot high water slides, rapids and whirlpools. There will be a cabaret bar and a caravan park, but no one, not even the Redcoats, will be allowed to say 'Hi-De-Hi' or 'Ho-De-Ho'. The famous fifty-year old catch-phrase is now officially banned by Butlin's.

SOMERWEST
WORLD
featuring
THE
SUNSPLASH
CLUB

Left, monorail at Skegness. Below, impression of the new Sunsplash club at redeveloped Minehead.

10 million adults in Great Britain have been to Butlin's.

Bill Butlin died 1980, and was buried in Jersey.

IT'S BYE-DE-BYE TO HI-DE-HI

Butlins bans telly catchphrase

EXCLUSIVE by MARTYN SHARPE

BUTLINS bosses have said the Hi-de-Hi catchphrase has got to Go-de-Go — because they're sick of hearing it in their holiday camps.

They reckon the famous chant from the BBC's popular show lowers the tone in their posh new "holiday centres."

Now Butlins own red-coats and visiting entertainers have been told to kiss it good-bye-de-bye.

A memo to managers at the company's six camps claim the routine re-creates "the image we've worked so hard to change."

Dated

But the end of Hi-de-Hi has left lots of entertainers feeling low-de-low!

Actor Paul Shane, who plays camp funny man Ted Bovis in the series,

Paul "people love shouting it out"

said yesterday: "Everybody likes shouting Hi-de-Hi.

"I don't know what they're going to do if people in the audience shout it. Are they going to ignore them?"

And TV comedian Freddie "Parrotface" Davies—who was a red-coat for five years — spluttered: "It's ludicrous! The phrase sums up holiday camps with their sense of fun and togetherness."

Another entertainer, who regularly works in Butlins camps, complained: "I've been shouting Hi-de-Hi since the TV show became a success, and the campers love to respond."

But at Butlins Bognor Regis HQ, operations manager Alan Ridgeway said: "We feel Hi-de-Hi has become a bit dated.

"The show is a slightly exaggerated view of what holiday camps were like in the 1950s and we are nothing like that now

"We would like to find a completely new phrase — if anyone has any ideas."

● Over to you, folks! Can you think up a suitable catchphrase for Butlins. Write to Hi-de-Hi, The Sun, 30 Bouverie Street, London EC4Y 8DE.

'Hi-de-Hi' obituary in *The Sun* newspaper.